REMINISCENCES.

REMINISCENCES

OF

Gibraltar, Egypt,

AND THE

Egyptian War, 1882.

(From the Ranks).

BY

JOHN PHILIP

(ABERDEEN CITY POLICE),

Late Sergeant,

2ND BATTALION DUKE OF CORNWALL'S LIGHT INFANTRY.

ABERDEEN: D. WYLLIE & SON.

1893.

AS A

TOKEN OF RESPECT AND ESTEEM

THIS LITTLE BOOK IS, WITH PERMISSION,

Dedicated

TO

MAJOR-GENERAL WILLIAM STEWART RICHARDSON, C.B.,

WHO, AS COLONEL, COMMANDED THE

2ND BATTALION DUKE OF CORNWALL'S LIGHT INFANTRY

DURING THE GREATER PART OF THE PERIOD

TREATED OF WITHIN ITS PAGES.

LETTERS.

Lord Napier of Magdala desires to express to Colonel Richardson and the officers, non-commissioned officers, and men of the Duke of Cornwall's Light Infantry, his satisfaction with their conduct and discipline during the time they have been under his command. Lord Napier of Magdala has much pleasure at being able to make a favourable report of the battalion to H.R.H. the Duke of Cambridge after the annual inspection, and he feels confident that it will fully maintain its honour and that of the country in the field.

Lord Napier of Magdala wishes the Regiment every success, and will watch its career with the greatest interest.

By order,

(Signed)   FRED SOLLY FLOOD,
Colonel,
A. A. General.

GIBRALTAR, 14th July, 1882.

BRIARWOOD,
SHAFTESBURY ROAD,
SOUTHSEA,
HANTS, 4th December, 1893.

Sergeant PHILIP,
 I have read with much interest your narrative on Gibraltar and the Egyptian Campaign of 1882, in which the 2nd Battalion Duke of Cornwall's Light Infantry took a prominent part.

I consider that your book will prove very interesting to all; but more especially to those who took an active part in such stirring scenes. I need hardly add that I feel proud to have my name associated with such a truthful record, and with pleasure I add my testimony as to the correctness of the details.

Believe me,
Yours very truly,
(Signed)   W. S RICHARDSON, C.B.,
Major-General,
Late Colonel Commanding 2nd Battalion Duke of Cornwall's Light Infantry.

Having served in the battalion, and been an eye-witness of most of the scenes which Sergeant Philip so graphically describes, I have much pleasure in testifying to the accuracy and truth of his sketches.

The little book should be of great interest, especially to all who belonged to the Regiment during that period of its history.

     (Signed) W. B. BROWNE,
         Lieut.-Colonel,
   Commanding 2nd Battalion Duke of Cornwall's
        Light Infantry.

BEGGARS' BUSH BARRACKS,
 DUBLIN, 11th Dec., 1893.

CONTENTS.

	PAGE
CHAPTER I.	
Arrival at Gibraltar and Celebration of the Queen's Birthday,	1
CHAPTER II.	
An Escapade in Spain,	13
CHAPTER III.	
Scenes and Recollections of the Rock,	19
CHAPTER IV.	
Off to the War: Arrival at Alexandria,	29
CHAPTER V.	
At Ramleh: Out-post Duty and Reconnoitring,	36
CHAPTER VI.	
En-route for Ismailia: Arrival at Ismailia,	44
CHAPTER VII.	
Fight at El-Magfar: Scene in a Melon Field,	53
CHAPTER VIII.	
With the Advanced Guard to Kassassin,	59
CHAPTER IX.	
Battle of Kassassin,	65

xiv.   *Contents.*

PAGE

CHAPTER X.

The Second Fight at Kassassin, ...   77

CHAPTER XI.

Battle of Tel-el-Kebir, ...   84

CHAPTER XII.

After the Battle, ...   92

CHAPTER XIII.

Cairo after the War; Grand March Past;
    Departure of the Holy Carpet, .   .   .   99

CHAPTER XIV.

The Pyramids of Egypt, ...   107

CHAPTER XV.

Recollections of Alexandria, ...   120

CHAPTER XVI.

Cholera at Alexandria; Arrival of Colonel
    Richardson, and Presentation of Egyptian
    Medals and Stars, ...   131

CHAPTER XVII.

Back to Cairo, ...   140

CHAPTER XVIII.

From Cairo to Assouan, ...   151

PREFACE.

THE author does not lay claim to be recounting any history save that of the movements of the Regiment to which he belonged, and the part it took in the Egyptian War of 1882.

A few scenes and reminiscences are selected from an eighteen months' stay on the Rock of Gibraltar, which the Regiment left to proceed to the shores of Egypt, taking with it the best wishes and confidence of the then Governor—that gallant soldier, Lord Napier of Magdala—as the letter kindly supplied by Major-General W. S. Richardson, C.B., and inserted on page ix., will testify.

The main portion of the book, however, deals with the historic land of Egypt, and the war there.

It has been my aim to carefully avoid entering into the reasons for or against this war, or from making any comment as to the cause or origin of it. All that can be found in the official history of the campaign.

Being present at the whole of the battles mentioned in this book, I have followed the fortunes of the Regiment through them in a narrative form, doing my best to depict the leading scenes and personal reminiscences as faithfully as my memory and note-book guide me. It must be borne in mind by the reader that a soldier in the ranks has not an opportunity of seeing all that takes place on a battlefield; therefore, I have only recorded what came under my own eye, borrowing none upon hearsay.

With regard to the part that deals exclusively with Egypt, it is formed on what a soldier would see while staying for a short time in the different towns. The habits, manners, religion, laws, and many other things connected with the people of Egypt, would require a longer stay and deeper study than a soldier can give while on a passing visit.

The whole object of this book is to give the reader as true and clear an idea of a soldier's life on the battle as well as the tented field, accompanied by a short account of outward sights in the streets of such towns as Gibraltar, Alexandria, and Cairo.

In my attempt at this, I have been fortunate in securing the approval of my late commanding officer, now Major-General W. S. Richardson, C.B., and the present commander of the 2nd Battalion Duke of Cornwall's Light Infantry, to whose letters in the foregoing pages I refer the reader for their opinion.

Hoping that the readers will find congenial reading, and, perhaps, a little information, is the wish of the author.

JOHN PHILIP.

ABERDEEN, December, 1893.

Reminiscences

OF

GIBRALTAR, EGYPT, AND THE EGYPTIAN WAR, 1882.

CHAPTER I.

ARRIVAL AT GIBRALTAR, AND CELEBRATION
OF QUEEN'S BIRTHDAY.

ON the 1st of January, 1881, I formed one of a draft of 140 men of the 32nd Regiment, or 1st Battalion Duke of Cornwall's Light Infantry, who mustered on the parade ground at Aldershot in readiness to proceed to Gibraltar to join the 2nd Battalion then stationed there. We had spent our last Christmas at home (for a long time to come) in a merry manner, with the Black Watch Royal Highlanders as our guests. Unfortunately for me that day, I was on guard duty, and so debarred from enjoying to the full the company of my countrymen. Though I had found my way into an English regiment, I was by birth an Aberdonian Scotchman. I will pass over the festivities between the two corps; in a word, suffice it to say that the carouse was long and deep, extending far into the night; in fact, the skirl of the bagpipes could be heard in the huts about 3 a.m. the following morning as some of the benighted pipers woke up from their potions, and, finding themselves still in the 32nd camp, treated their English comrades to a few bars of Scotch music before they trooped off to their own quarters.

This morning, New-Year's Day, when Scotchmen make merry, our gallant friends of the Black Watch were to pay back the compliment. Such scenes of fraternity among regiments spread a wonderful bond of friendship, for, after a few years, it was my fortune to meet the same corps in Egypt, and what was begun in Aldershot was resumed there. On account of our departure, which would prevent us being present at the arranged feast, the Highlanders had set their minds on giving us something to keep out the cold. Long before the "reveille" sounded, several of them were stealthily stealing through our lines, whisky bottle in hand, and, on the sly, we had "our morning," the last glass on British soil for many a day. Though the morning was cold, and snow on the ground, a number of troops had turned out to see us off, the 32nd being a popular regiment in camp. Amid the cheers of our friends and the lively music of the band, we marched on our way to the railway station, and, before night, were safely on board Her Majesty's troop ship, "Himalaya," at Portsmouth, bound for the Rock of Gibraltar.

I will not dwell on the voyage, which, after the first pangs of sea-sickness were allayed, proved to be of a pleasant character, and the fifth day saw us safe and sound in the Bay of Gibraltar. Our vessel steamed alongside the New Mole Wharf, where we disembarked, and marched through an archway on to an open square, surrounded by massive pieces of ordnance, such as we had never seen before. The commanding officer of our new

Celebration of Queen's Birthday. 3

regiment met us there, and conducted us through the street to our future quarters, known as the Wellington Front Barracks. After being portioned off to different companies, and had partaken of a few drinks at the canteen, we were quite at home with our henceforth comrades, and a jolly lot they were.

I was much struck with this mighty fortress, and, for the benefit of those who have never seen it, I will briefly describe the rougher outlines as it appeared to me at first sight. Beginning at the south end overlooking the entrance to the Mediterranean, the rock rises almost perpendicular from the blue waters to a great height; while on the top, and here and there on the way up, frowning down on the tumultuous sea, are several batteries of enormous cannon. Skimming the eye along the jagged top for about a mile, it reaches the signal station, from where all passing vessels are hailed, and also where the time-gun is fired, calling on the gate-keeper to open or shut the gates, which is done with as much care as a jeweller would shut his shop door. The back part of the rock, or rather the side next the Mediterranean, also rises nearly perpendicular, and is fortified by nature without the aid of the machines of man. On the west side, looking down on the spacious bay, where the fleets of all nations often repose, stands the thickly-populated town of Gibraltar—a mass of narrow winding streets, which, owing to the incline they are built on, are perforce connected by big flights of stone stairs. Between the town and the south end lie the gardens and promenades, the loveliness and beauty of which are undreamt of here. Geraniums grow in wild profusion, their bright blooms mixing with beautiful tropical plants giving a delightful and almost paradisal look to the scene. The north end, which overlooks the plain connecting the rock with Spain, stands straight and smooth from the land till it reaches the height of 1350 feet. Away up in the face of the perpendicular mass of solid rock are hewn the famous galleries, whose dark mouths can be seen in regular rows; while hidden in those recesses, ready for action, are the iron monsters of war, by whose power Britain holds her sway over this coveted fortress. Away up on the topmost point is a battery of six or eight guns, known as the Sky Battery. There are three entrances to the rock, two by water and one by land, all formed by long and narrow archways, with a draw-bridge behind, and at sunrise and sundown every day, with exact regularity, a sergeant may be seen carrying a large bunch of keys, and guarded by a soldier on either side with fixed bayonets, passing from entrance to entrance, blocking, with the aid of machines, those passages, by raising the bridge outside against the mouth of the arch, leaving a broad ditch behind, thus cutting off all ingress or egress till morning light, when they again return to open them for the next day's business.

The streets are thickly set with wine shops, some of them small, dark hovels; others, more for the use of the numerous garrison, are large, and fitted up with captivating grandeur, and furnished internally with a stage, whereon, in the evening, artistes are engaged to amuse the audience by song and dance. Sometimes the amusement is enlivened by the introduction of some of the rougher style of theatrical plays. Those latter places are generally crowded with soldiers and sailors, mixed with a sprinkling of the better class of civilians, for the army and navy are there looked upon with respect.

The lower ten prefer the unsavoury odour of the darker dens.

Although freely patronising the over-abundant wine shops, the natives are by no means a drunken lot, as it is a rare sight to see a rock scorpion (a sobriquet bestowed on natives of the Rock) staggering hilariously through the streets with that idiotic and devil-may-care air peculiar to those who have allowed John Barleycorn to take possession of the upper storey.

With regard to the fair sex, I may say that I hardly ever saw any of them intoxicated during my stay of $1\frac{1}{2}$ years there, except when the British soldier or sailor got on the loose, and persuaded some of those dark-eyed beauties to share too deeply with them the contents of the flowing bowl. Lewd women there were in abundance, but they were relegated to a part of the town by themselves, and those encountering them had themselves to blame for being in that locality, as those ladies of pleasure (as they were styled) dare not leave their own street in pursuit of their calling.

The whole (or mostly so) of the inhabitants were of the Spanish type, speaking a sort of guttural Spanish, but, nevertheless, proficient in the English language. If one of them was engaged in conversation with you, and a civilian neighbour joined, they instantly changed into their own dialect—a rather tantalising process, as you found yourself quite at sea; you might actually be the subject of discourse for all you knew.

Here a soldier's life undergoes a complete change from the continual drill and barrack scrubbing indulged in, sometimes to an excessive extent, at home. There were numerous guards to mount every day; in fact, the outer lines of the rock bristled with sentries, their red coats and shining bayonets being encountered at every turn. A martial air pervades the whole place, cannons here, there, and everywhere. Even the inhabitants are under the stern rule of martial law. Soldiers, on duty along with the civil police, patrol the streets after nightfall, and every person, both high and low, found moving about after 11 p.m. without a written permission from the town major are indiscriminately "run in" to the main guard, and from there (if civilians) passed on to the police office.

Besides the guard and picket duty, plenty of manual labour is always to be got. Every day large working parties from the different regiments are employed on some part of the ever-changing fortifications, sometimes renewing, sometimes demolishing; it matters not to the soldier as long as he receives his 3d. or 4d. per hour, which is the allotted pay over and above his regimental allowance. A drill now and again, with an occasional field-day at the "North Front" (the designation of the neck of land joining the rock to Spain), completes the ordinary routine of a soldier's work at Gib.

Our amusements consisted of what could be obtained in the recreation rooms, such as billiards, draughts, dominoes, reading, &c., or drinking and song-singing in the canteen; sometimes off to visit companions in other regiments, or meandering about the streets, and spending an hour or two in the drinking and amusement saloons. There was no such thing as proceeding Spain-wards for the private soldier, as only non-commissioned officers were granted that privilege, and them only by a pass from the town major. People unacquainted with the stern military discipline of Gibraltar might say, why not take a trip across the line without leave, for a broad road, about ¾ of a mile long, stretched right along the centre of the level plain which lay between us and sunny Spain; but this was a difficult matter. On no other part of this land, except the road, was human being allowed to cross (barring the governor, then Lord Napier of Magdala). A line of British sentries were posted from sea to sea, with strict injunctions, as strictly carried out, to prevent any person from crossing or recrossing, except by the proper track, and it was forbidden to privates.

About 800 yards in front of our sentries was a similar line of Spanish soldiers following out the same instructions: therefore we were confined within the sea-and-gun-girt walls of Gibraltar. Nevertheless, we managed to make the rock a lively habitation, and taking all in all, before I left I had a decided liking for it and its people.

The first event of importance that took place during my sojourn was the celebration of the Queen's birthday.

By the 1st of May it was the talk of the town, the citizens looking forward to it with lively interest, much more so than do the citizens of Queen Victoria's own land. All seemed to be striving to make the town gay with decorations, for, in the principal thoroughfares, the work of beautifying began about a week before the auspicious occasion, which I will now briefly describe.

At 5 a.m., on the 24th May, 1881, the loud boom of of the time-gun broke the stillness of a clear and unclouded morning, and, ere its echoes had died away among the neighbouring hills of Spain and Morocco, the royal standard could be seen fluttering in the gentle breeze from the flagstaff of the Sky Battery, the highest point of the gigantic Rock. Down below in the town all was soon bustle and stir, the citizens vieing with each other in the amount of gay and many-coloured flags and bunting they could display. By 10 a.m. the principal streets were one grand mass of decorations. From roof to roof, and from window to window, stretched lines and arches of gorgeous flowers, surmounted by richly embroidered flags and ribbons. Underneath thronged the inhabitants and visitors in holiday attire. Spanish and Italian beauties, with their graceful mantillas over their shapely heads, men with broad-brimmed sombreros and swarthy faces, mingled in picturesque confusion with the bright scarlet coats of the line regiments and the blue uniform of the Royal Artillery. The garb of Old Gaul was not wanting, as a Highland regiment formed part of the garrison. Passing through this gay throng, one could hear the Spanish, Italian, and English languages, and occasionally the broad vernacular of the Scot, as the lads of the kilt and plaid mingled with the crowd. Altogether it was a bright and animated sight, and presented a great contrast to 10 a.m. in the Granite City, where, with the exception of a flag here and there, nothing could be seen to show a stranger that the celebration of the birthday of the greatest monarch on earth was in progress. But the saying is, a prophet has no honour in his own country, and truly this would go so far as to affect even Queen Victoria, judging from outward appearance. But the inhabitants of the two places are different, and the quiet joy of the Aberdonians may be equally as true and deep as that of their more effusive and passionate brethren on the rock.

At twelve noon the real rejoicing began, for as soon as the first stroke of twelve tolled from the town clock, a white puff of smoke could be seen far away up on the topmost point of the Rock, followed immediately after by the report of the first gun firing the royal salute. This was the signal for a general fusillade, battery after battery adding its tribute to royalty. The guards were turned out, and stood at the "present arms" until the guns had ceased firing. In the spacious bay lay quietly at anchor during the forenoon the monsters of the Mediterranean fleet, accompanied by several foreign war and other vessels of different nationalities, all gaily decorated from stem to stern; and now, with yards manned by "gallant tars," those noble vessels were vieing with the batteries on shore in paying tribute to Britain and her Sovereign. Report after report rang from their solid decks, and as the white smoke curled and twined through the tall masts and spars and brilliant decorations on its upward way, it was indeed a noble sight for Britons to behold. Nor were the foreign ships behind: they were also sending forth their share of fire and smoke, and for a quarter of an hour the bay was one roar of artillery. In the barracks all were on the *qui vive*, and cheer after cheer came heartily from lusty throats, which had to be slacked immediately after in the canteen.

At 1.30 the Governor of the neighbouring province of Spain arrived to attend the review of the troops that was to be held later on. He was received at the Waterport Jetty by a guard of honour of the Highlanders, and drove to the Governor of Gibraltar's house, where he was again received by a guard of honour, this time of my own regiment, the 2nd Battalion Duke of Cornwall's Light Infantry. As he drove up, the band played the general salute, and the guard presented arms. The white-haired general doffed his cap and bowed low until the last strains of the salute died away, and then he passed into the house to be the guest of the Governor of the Rock until the review hour.

About 4.30 p.m. each regiment mustered on its own parade ground, and, leaving only sufficient men to look after the barracks, commenced their march to the " North

Front." The way out of the Rock was by the principal street through a barrack square, then through an arch: about 50 yards long, thence by a broad road with water on both sides for about 100 yards, and we arrive at the drill ground, which consists of the level piece of land that joins the rock to Spain. As regiment after regiment filed through the streets underneath the bright arches of flowers to the stirring strains of their bands, crowds of spectators gathered and followed, evidently bent on seeing the grand parade, but more especially the firing of the *feu de joie*. Arrived on the grounds, the troops were drawn up in two lines about fifty yards apart. I was on special duty near the saluting point, and had a splendid view of the whole scene. Directly in front of me were the solid lines of British troops with their faces to the Gibraltar Bay and their backs to the blue waves of the Mediterranean. On the right were the blue-coated artillery with their field guns, next to them came the serried ranks of the Highlanders, and away to the left were the scarlet coats and white facings of my own corps. The second line was entirely composed of English regiments. To the left of the whole line, and about 400 yards off, towering hundreds of feet above, was the rugged and almost perpendicular end of the Rock which guarded this the only entrance by land.

Punctually at the appointed time, the Governor of Gibraltar and his guest, escorted by a troop of Spanish cavalry, came dashing on the ground, and were received with a salute, after which the two generals rode along and inspected the ranks, and then came the signal for the *feu de joie*. The guns from the Sky Battery began, and they were followed by those in the galleries this time sending forth their voice in turn. The cannonade ran slowly along the whole of the embrasures, some of them hidden by trees and foliage. Nothing could be seen but the smoke slowly curling over their tops. Standing where we were, one could form an idèa of the impregnability of this fortress when the very nature of the Rock lent her shape to engineer's skill. When the firing subsided on the Rock it was taken up by the artillery on the right, and from them the line picked it up, and, as the sharp rattle of the musketry ran along those thin red lines tipped with steel, the scene was so grand that the spectators could not suppress their excitement, and gave vent to a cheer. When the firing ceased, the Governor and his guest rode forward, and the former, taking off his plumed hat, called for three cheers for the Queen. Every soldier in the ranks took off his helmet, and, holding it aloft in his right hand, a deafening cheer was sent up from 5000 British throats. The spectators also joined, and the band played the National Anthem. The Spanish Governor sat on his horse with his head uncovered and bowed low, and there remained until the music ceased, and then he resumed his upright seat. A march past followed, and, as each company passed the saluting point, they were greeted with cheers by the assembled multitude, more notably when the Highlanders went sweeping past to the tune of the "Highland Laddie" on the bagpipes. We then marched back to the barracks, and each man was supplied with a pint of beer to drink Her Majesty's health. This was done, and in many cases several more "pinties" were sent after it, as a proof of extra loyalty. At any rate, the walls of the old canteen of the Duke of Cornwall's Light Infantry resounded with mirth and song until the bugle sounded to "shut up." In the town the inhabitants paraded the streets in jovial crowds playing melodeons, their favourite outside instrument. Dances were arranged in close and green, and all made merry as becometh the great occasion. Such is a Queen's birthday in Gibraltar.

CHAPTER II.

AN ESCAPADE IN SPAIN.

SHORTLY after this I was promoted to the rank of corporal, and having had a longing eye on the neighbouring Spanish town for a considerable time, one Sunday morning in the month of July saw me on horseback, accompanied by a chum, careering along the broad road, bound for the cork woods of Spain. The horses we had were hired for the day at a cost of 2 dollars (8/-) each. Some might say we ought to have chosen a more lawful day for our excursion; but Sunday was the day we could get best clear of work and duties, so it was generally set aside for rambling.

Early in the bracing morning air we passed both English and Spanish sentries (showing our passes to the former) through the town of Lena, thence along the sands of the bay for about a mile, and then bearing off to our right we made straight for the white walls of San Roque, a town of small dimensions, situated on a hill within sight of, and some eight miles from, the nearest part of British territory. Our journey on this our first trip proved a failure, for the horse I was riding got fairly lame, and we had to stable up for the day, and enjoy ourselves as we best could at San Roque. There is a sight to be seen at the entrance to this town (I am glad to say) totally unknown in our own land. For the last few hundred yards we had to pick our way through hundreds of invalid and deformed beggars, who even crawled in front of our horses beseeching alms. If they got trod upon, we knew a great outcry would arise, bringing the gendarmes on the scene, and 10 to 1 we would be marched off to jail without ceremony. Stabling up our horses at a large and well-furnished hotel, we sauntered forth to look around us.

Owing to the hill on which this town was constructed, the streets had mostly all a sharp incline. They were paved with large round boulders, and with the grass growing up between them. A deserted look hung about it; no vehicles of any description did I see. The whole traffic seemed to be conducted through the medium of pack mules, of which there were abundance. The few inhabitants we saw were apparently familiar with red coats visiting, as they took little notice of us, further than an inquisitive glance in passing.

We wended our way to the barracks, and got into conversation with a soldier (more by signs than by words, for we could not understand each other), who invited us to have a look inside, which invitation we accepted. The soldiers were all seated on the floor round a big pot containing beans or something of that sort, each one taking a spoonful in turn. We were asked to join the circle, but declined by a shake of the head (which seemed to mean "no" over all the earth.) The sight of this meagre dinner, and the barely-furnished and miserable room, gave us cause to be thankful that we were British soldiers instead of Spanish. This scene presented a great contrast compared with our neatly-arranged abodes—the soldiers seated at a long table, all trim and neat, with a pound of roast beef and potatoes before them. Leaving the barracks, we sauntered aimlessly through the streets, and, beginning to feel the pangs of hunger, we resolved to ask the first persons we met for some place wherein we could get a good repast. Two lovely black-eyed damsels were coming in our direction, and we made ready to try our best Spanish on them, which consisted of a few common words we had heard on the Rock till they were familiar. The maidens seemed greatly to enjoy our attempts to imitate their language, to judge from their merry laughter, when, by signs and grunts, I made them understand that the inner man required attention. They promptly picked up our wants, and, giving us the signal to accompany them, we soon entered a neat little house, not very far from the inn where our steeds were stabled. It proved to be their parents' abode, who made us heartily welcome, and, could we have understood each other's dialects, a more jolly afternoon might have been spent. As it was, a huge decanter of wine (the favourite Spanish beverage) was produced, a big omelet at once made, and we and our fair companions were in a short time seated, in high spirits, at a good meal. By and by a lady friend arrived who could both speak and understand English, and she took up the role of interpreter. When we left to hurry back to the Rock before gun-fire, we had promised to return that day four weeks to spend another happy afternoon with our new and charming friends.

True to our promise, the fourth Sunday found us again on horseback galloping gaily across the border. This time we had two sound and fleet steeds, for we had given the hirer a good blowing up for supplying us with such poor animals on the last occasion. Past San Roque we went, and ran right into the cork woods, about six miles further off. Soon after entering those woods we came to a number of paths branching off in different directions. Not knowing which one to follow, we threw the reins over our horses' necks, and allowed them to choose for themselves. They took the wrong one, and instead of arriving at the place we wanted, viz., a rest known as "The Long Stables," we found ourselves standing in the yard of a convent. Seeing some of the nuns looking out at the windows, we signed to them that we wanted food for both horse and man, but they hid themselves away. Driving our horses into a house bearing a slight resemblance to a stable, we gave them some grass which was lying there. For about half-an-hour we hung about this convent, in hopes that some one would come and get payment for our stabling, but no; so we mounted and rode back to where the paths diverged, and, following another for about a mile, we reached the Long Stables.

Here we got a good breakfast, our horses fed, and after an hour's ramble in the woods, we again mounted and retraced our steps to San Roque to see our sweethearts, who were, to all appearance, overjoyed to again meet us. The fairest of the two had been taken possession of by my chum, and she seemed to be deeply in love with him, as I heard the same interpreter we had on the last visit tell him point blank that the girl wanted to marry him. He, not thinking on the consequences, no doubt taking the whole affair as a joke, readily complied, and, in a bantering tone, said he would be ready when he came back. There was no formalities gone through, not even a name asked, and on the way home he was laughing about the idea of marrying a girl who could not understand a word he said, nor she him. Both of us had taken it as a joke, but we were soon to get our eyes opened.

Five weeks after was the appointed day of our next meeting, and, after a run to the Long Stables, and a few hours' enjoyment in the green woods, we posted back to pay our promised visit to our lady loves at San Roque. But something was in the air. As we entered, we were both greeted with an even greater show of affection than on the previous occasion, especially my companion. A number of young men and maidens were gathered together, among them a young fellow who could speak and understand English fairly well. He was not long in telling us that a priest was coming to arrange the preliminaries for my companion's marriage. This was a dilemma; how were we to get out of it? Nothing was further from my chum's thoughts than marrying this Spanish beauty, and, with the perspiration standing in beads on his forehead, he whispered to me, "What shall we do?" I whispered back, "Pocket our courage and run for it. You go and saddle the horses and be ready; I will stop to allay suspicion." At this moment the door opened, and a priest entered, and, in the confusion of hand-shaking and greeting, my chum slipped out. He was not more than five minutes gone ere his lovely bride missed him. I had to explain that he was away to see after the feeding of the horses, but as he was staying too long I would go and bring him back. Whether it was by the guilty look on my face as I went out, I know not, but I had not gone far when, on looking round, I saw four of the young men following after me. There was nothing for it now but a bold dash, and away I ran. The horses were standing saddled and bridled, and my companion mounted. I sprang into the saddle, and off without even getting time to fix my feet in the stirrups, for an angry crowd was close at my heels, attracted by the chase.

We rode at a mad gallop for about two miles, and then, seeing we were not pursued, broke into a slower pace.

My friend was thankful for his deliverance; but, for three weeks or so, he said he was the owner of an uneasy mind, in case his would-be bride found him out in the regiment. However, we heard no more of it, and you may be sure we kept the occurrence solely to ourselves. Had it broken out among our comrades, we would have lived in torment for long. As it was, we never trusted ourselves on Spanish soil again.

CHAPTER III.

SCENES AND RECOLLECTIONS OF THE ROCK.

I DO not intend to weary the reader with any of the details of the ordinary every-day life of a soldier in Gibraltar, as they would prove uninteresting and weary. Therefore I will only record briefly a few recollections which may prove acceptable, and then pass on to sterner scenes.

A few months after our escapade in Spain, a new bishop was appointed to minister to the spiritual affairs of the Rock residenters.

The British Government seemed to have chosen one against the wishes of the majority of the inhabitants, for as soon as the name was published in the *Gibraltar Chronicle*, the daily official paper, a great outcry arose, and for weeks the natives could not conceal their bitter feelings. When they met in the streets and drinking saloons, their sole topic of conversation turned on the appointment of the new bishop; and openly they threatened that they would resist the ordination to the last. It looked as if that day was to be a day of bloodshed, for many of the inhabitants went the length of saying that revolvers were provided, and they would try our mettle before we forced a man on them against their wishes. Whether it was that the governor, Lord Napier, heard of these threats, and thinking it would be a bad precedent for Gibraltar to allow its inhabitants to think for one moment that they could cope with the garrison, I know not; but the order went forth that, on a certain day, at a certain hour, the ordination was to take place in a chapel situated in the very centre of the town.

On the morning of the appointed day the whole population were early astir. The male portion seemed disinclined to go to work, and stood in groups at the street corners with sour and down-cast faces, waiting the turn of events. Not till twelve noon did the troops receive any orders, and then they came—short, sharp, and decisive. " Fall in ; on your barrack squares ; serve out ten rounds of ammunition per man, and wait for further instructions." While this order was being carried out the gates of the Rock were shut, and all communication from the outer world cut off. The inhabitants were alone with the garrison.

A few companies of different regiments were marched to commanding places in the streets, and a battalion took up a position in front of the chapel, on a large square near the main guard and police office. About one p.m. Lord Napier arrived, accompanied by several officers and gentlemen, among them the obnoxious bishop. Proceeding towards the door of the chapel they found it secured, and the noise issuing from the interior indicated that it had been taken possession of by some of the bolder inhabitants. The Governor conversed a few minutes with his staff, and then a body of military police was called forward, who, with massive wooden beams, soon shattered the door. A low murmur of discontent ran through a large crowd gathered near by, which was instantly suppressed by the stern order to disperse as a body of troops advanced and drove them off. On entering the chapel, the tongue of the large bell was hurled at the military police, and, as it rang on the door step, without hitting anyone, Lord Napier called out. " halt!" The police stopped in the doorway, and now it could be seen that the Governor's blood was up. He promptly gave the order for two lines of troops to be formed up, facing each other with fixed bayonets, about six paces apart, and extending from the chapel door to the door of the police station, a distance of about 150 yards. When this was completed, the sharp command, "charge bayonets!" was heard, and as the bayonet points came down, a blank space of about three yards was only left between the rows of glistening steel. The next command was to the military police to clear the chapel of its invaders, and in they rushed with a will, and as the besieged were driven out one after another, they staggered back aghast at the sight of the bristling lane of steel, and the dark open door at the opposite end. There was no loop-hole of escape. Down that lane every one of them passed, and found themselves under lock and key. The bishop was then installed without more trouble. The stern measures taken with the ringleaders effectually cooled the ardour of the onlookers. The following day some 30 of the leading citizens were picked out of the 80 or 90 who were locked up, and sent to prison for periods ranging from thirty days to six months. They were escorted through the streets to prison by a company of troops with fixed bayonets, but no attempt at rescue was made. From subsequent events it seemed that Lord Napier simply wanted to demonstrate clearly that the orders of Britain were supreme, for the whole of the offending citizens were released in about a fortnight, and the bishop removed to some other place. With this lesson taken to heart, things soon assumed their old friendly shape.

About the time of the above occurrence, I was selected for one of the numerous posts of Government employment largely filled by soldiers, and known as " staff jobs." My work consisted of looking after the landing of boats, taking note of cargoes, and, generally speaking, keeping everything in proper order on a wharf immediately outside the landward gate of the Rock.

My only connection with the regiment while so employed was that I wore uniform, and slept in the barracks. I left every morning at gun-fire, and did not return till the shutting of the gates at night. I took my rations with me, and, having a wooden hut to stay in, rigged up with a stove inside, I managed to cook my own food.

Now, our then colonel, under whatever circumstances, always liked to see his men trig and clean, and often sauntered round to those on employment, away from the regiment to have a look at their appearance. Well, one morning, about two months after I had commenced my duties on the wharf, I (feeling rather hungrier than usual, and also having a comrade with me whom I had invited to breakfast) walked into a blacksmith's shop near by, where I was well acquaint, on purpose to do my cooking—by this means saving me the trouble of lighting my own fire, as I happened to be in a lazy mood.

The grimy atmosphere of the smithy made it undesirable for me to don my best coat, so I substituted for it a dirty old threadbare tunic. I had invested in two red herrings and four eggs, and, when my cooking was over, I emerged from the shop carrying a black canteen full of coffee in one hand, while in the other I bore a plate whereon lay my herrings and eggs. I would have been almost g'ad had the earth opened and swallowed me up, for I no sooner breathed the open air than I was face to face with our stern old colonel mounted on horseback, and accompanied by one of his daughters. My hands being full, I could not receive him with the usual military sa'ute, and I knew I was in for it. I expected, at least, to get a severe rebuke for this unsoldier-like appearance in public, when, judge of my surprise, he saluted me with " Corporal, how are matters getting on with you ? " I replied, " Very well, sir," and was moving backwards in hopes that he would pass on, which he did ; but he called on me to follow him as he wanted to speak to me, and he had no time to stop his horse. Reluctantly I obeyed, and along the road we went—he sitting on his horse with a broad smile on his face, I following up alongside with my plate of herrings and eggs in one hand, and the black canteen in the other. The eggs rolled on the plate, and it was with difficulty that I got them to stay there. The road was crowded with passers-by, whose smothered and sometimes open laughter jarred on my ears. For fully 200 yards through those crowds of natives and soldiers I tramped, and then, taking compassion on me, with a merry twinkle in his eye, the colonel bade me go back, and hoped he had read me a lesson never to appear outside in such an unbecoming manner again. My blood was boiling with inward indignation at the spectacle I must have presented to the onlookers, and, dashing the plate to the earth, I literally pounded the herrings and eggs into pulp on the hard road, and went back to my own hut to partake of a more frugal breakfast—a sadder but a wiser man.

Misfortunes, people say, do not come singly, and so it proved with me.

In little more than a week I was fished out of the deep waters of the bay, and worse still, for about a fortnight after, I had to nurse two sprained wrists. The accident happened in this manner : My duties rendered it necessary for me sometimes to sail in a small skiff about the jetty to regulate the anchoring of the fishing crafts. One forenoon, after this task was completed, I being in a working humour, pulled away across the bay to view a foreign man-of-war lying a short distance off.

There are numerous old hulks in the bay used as coal stores, there being no room on shore for such storage.

As my tiny craft emerged from behind the black timbers of one of those, I heard a cry of many voices, and on looking in that direction, a pleasure boat with sails set was within 12 yards of me, splashing through the water at a fast rate. We were too near each other for any of us to avoid a collision. I had just time to jump to my feet, and, without thinking on what I was doing, held out both my hands as if to stop the on-coming boat. Against my hands she dashed with tremendous force, pitching me clean overboard, and, as I sank, I heard the noise of her keel swishing through the water above my head. I could swim very little, and on coming, breathless and dazed, to the surface, I had just sufficient presence of mind to try and keep afloat. The boat that did the deed turned, and in a few minutes I was taken safely on board. They offered to convey me on shore, but I preferred to go into my own skiff, which was floating close by, untouched by the collision. With many apologies, mostly in Spanish, they acceded to my request, and picking up my oars and handing them to me, they waved their adieus. It was now that I felt the result of the blow I had received. My arms would not work the oars, and before I landed I was sick with pain. Next day I had both hands tied to my head in a large arm-sling. The superintendent of the wharf sent his son, a boy of 14, to do my writing work, and between us we managed to keep things going till I was cured ; but the recollection of that fearful crash on my arms remains vivid in my memory, and also the madness of the unaccountable thought that prompted me to imagine that the puny strength of a human arm could have stopped the onward course of that heavy boat, driven by its broad sheets of canvas spread to a rattling breeze.

Seeing that I have taken the readers with me on my dip into the waters of the bay, before leaving let me also take them for a dip into the interior of the rock.

High up, near the top, is situated the Cave of Saint Michael, and one day, along with a few companions, I set off to visit it. We climbed up the steep, winding, and rugged path for about an hour ere we arrived at the dark-looking entrance of the cavern. We found a soldier belonging to a Highland regiment stationed there, one of whose duties it was to show visitors the wonders of the place. When so employed, he was in the best of humour, the loneliness of his post making him gladly welcome whoever came to see him. He could speak for hours about the mysteries of this cave and the grand men whom he had guided through it. I remember that he was very much disappointed that he had no torches at the time, so that, with the reflection of their flaming light, we might see it in all its glory and splendour. He also turned out to be a " townee " of mine (a slang name used when parties come from the same town or countryside). "Townees," when they meet in foreign lands, generally fraternise with each other, and get friendly as they talk of youthful romps in their native place, and so did we.

Entering a large dark hole, we found ourselves in a

wide roomy chamber. Masses of congealed stone hung from the roof, resembling huge icicles in shape and confusion of form, but the colour was light brown and grey, with a silvery sparkle intermixed. The walls were also clothed in the same ornamental manner. Even with the feeble blink of lighted candles which we carried the place had a beautiful look, and we could imagine the effect under the bright glare of torches. Passing on, we went through a narrow passage, and emerged into a smaller chamber than the first, but more magnificent. Stalactites hung, not only from the roof in all conceivable shapes, but several of them had, in the length of ages, extended till they reached the floor, forming pillars moulded by nature into the most lovely curves and pinnacles, their very irregularity adding to the beauty of the place, which brought to my mind the enchanted caves of Arabian Nights fame. Down we went until we reached a small hole, into which our soldier guide went, and I followed—the remainder of the party staying behind. Owing to the smallness of this hole, it was with difficulty that I got through. My companion, though a bigger man than me, was a long way ahead, and evidently getting on with little trouble. I suppose he had scrambled through so often that the passage was used to his burly frame, or else his frame was used to the passage. I was thankful when I stood beside him at the other end of this crevice in a roomier space. For about 30 yards we trod carefully on through passages, sometimes narrow, sometimes high and broad—roofs and walls covered with the fantastically natural sculptured stone—until we arrived at the limit of penetration. Close in front of us was a yawning precipice—its depths hidden in unutterable darkness.

By this time I should think we were at least 80 yards

Scenes and Recollections of the Rock. 27

into the very heart of the rock, and further we dare not go. My companion told me that once on a time long ago an attempt had been made to fathom the depth of the black gulf that now barred our further progress, but those who went down never came back. As to the truth of this I cannot say.

There is another legend connected with this place, but, speaking for myself, I do not believe it. However, I will give it the reader, as I heard it on several occasions at Gib. It runs so : A number of monkeys have their abode away up in the face of the rock, near the cave. They are well cared for and fed by the soldier who guided us. Rumour has it that on several occasions these well-fed animals have disappeared, and the same ones have been captured across the Straits in Africa. Now, the mystery is, how did they get there, by a subterranean passage, the beginning of which is St. Michael's Cave. So say some of the would-be wise men of the Rock ; but, if such is the case, it has baffled man as yet to find it, and will do so, I am afraid, to the end of time.

To retrace our steps was the next thought, as the want of air made breathing difficult. For the same cause our candles almost refused to burn. On reaching the large chamber near the mouth of the cave, our guide drew our attention to the ends of the stone icicles, where we saw numerous (what seemed to be) soft, woolly balls stuck thereon. It proved to be bats, hanging in hundreds. I reached up and p'ucked off about 20, putting them into my helmet, and out we went. Very soon they began to be lively in their prison, screeching and walloping about on my head, so that I had to give up the idea of taking them to barracks as I intended. It would never do to go through the streets with such a disturbance going on about my cranium. I therefore lifted my helmet, and away they whirled, some going tilt against the hard rock in their hurry, others skimming away through the air, were soon lost to sight. We wended our way back to the barracks, highly pleased with our afternoon's exploration.

CHAPTER IV.

OFF TO THE WAR: ARRIVAL AT ALEXANDRIA.

IME rolled quietly and smoothly on till the month of June, 1882, when the daily papers conveyed to us rumours of an expected outbreak of war in Egypt. All was excitement, for we knew that we would be about the first to proceed there, being fully up to war strength and seasoned to heat—the regiment having been previously stationed at Bermuda.

Day after day the papers were eagerly scanned, and on the 12th July came the news of the bombardment of Alexandria, which took place on the preceding day. Almost simultaneously came the order for us to embark on Her Majesty's troopship "Malabar" for Egypt. Little time was lost, and, two days after the order was received, we were standing in the barrack square ready to march. Crowds of people gathered to see us off, and there was weeping and wailing among the married women, some of whom had almost to be torn from their husband's embrace. As if to further outrage their feelings, the command, "quick march!" was quickly followed by the band playing the "Girl I Left Behind." Very soon we were comfortably berthed on board the good old trooper, and, amid ringing cheers from the multitude gathered on the quay, we steamed away from Gibraltar.

Passing through the gut, we were met by H.M. ship "Baccahante," on board of which the young Princes then were, and the sailors, instinctively knowing, by the state of affairs in Egypt, that we were bound for the war, manned the yards and cheered as we passed. We returned the cheer with equal heartiness, for we were all on the *qui vive* with excitement.

There was only the one regiment on board, and we had plenty of room to reel about. The captain relaxed the usual rigorous discipline observed on a troop-ship, I suppose on account of us being bound for active service; in fact, he said to some fellows who were rather boisterous that he would not be bothered with them again; their days were numbered—anything but a cheering assurance. Favoured with splendid weather, full steam ahead, and sails bellowed out by a light breeze, our gallant ship bore us as rapidly on, and on the fifth day we arrived at Malta. Something must be wrong, for here we were ordered to disembark, and disembark we did that very night, and took up our quarters in barracks. We lay down for the night on the floor of the empty rooms, thoroughly out of spirits.

Early in the morning the work of furnishing began: bed-ticks, barrack furniture, and all the necessary utensils were drawn from the quartermaster's stores. We were all busily employed getting things into ship-shape order when, about 10 A.M., the bugles sounded for colour-sergeants. Instantly work was stopped. Somehow or other we instinctively knew that it was needless to proceed, and all eyes were directed at the returning colour-sergeants, and a hearty hurrah rang out as they gave the order, carry back the barracks' furniture, "boys," and fall-in in two hours for Egypt. The quartermaster had to take in his stores faster than he gave them out, and by the appointed time we were again on board the "Malabar."

Arrival at Alexandria. 31

This time the voyage was no sinecure, for, with the half of the 35th Regiment and a number of artillerymen, we were packed like sardines in a box. The upper part of the vessel bore a warlike aspect : guns were placed on the fore-deck, while along the sides were ranged vehicles of different descriptions—water-carts, luggage-carts, ammunition waggons, &c. The sailors pushed their way through us with bent heads and bare feet, and the continual cry of gangway (make room) was heard on every hand.

For three days we bowled merrily over the swelling waves of the Mediterranean, and on the fourth day—the 24th day of July, 1882—we expected to sight the historic shores of Egypt. By mid-day all eyes were strained, eagerly skimming the horizon in front for the first glimpse of land. About 4 p m., the cry was heard, "Land ahead!" and at once there was a rush for the fore-deck.

On to the top of gun-carriages, carts, &c., we climbed, the naval officers yelling to us to keep down; but they did not seem anxious to enforce their order, as those who did not come off at the first bidding were allowed to stay, and those who came down were not long till they clambered up again. Sure enough, the low-lying land could be distinguished not many miles away ; so flat was it that it looked almost level with the sea. As we nearer and nearer drew, several noble mansions were seen standing among groves of palm and other trees on our right, about half-a-mile inland. In front of us rose the numerous minerats and domes (so common in eastern towns) of the ancient and unfortunate city of Alexandria ; while between us and it, reclining on the still bosom of the mighty deep, were the ships of the Mediterranean fleet. Several foreign war vessels were also lying in the bay, but the British flag predominated.

The scene was quiet and magnificent: not a sound was to be heard save the thumping of the engines of the "Malabar," and the swish of the water as she glided on. It was hardly credible that the same setting sun, whose rays of silvery light were sparkling on the glassy sea and dancing among the graceful spars of those mighty ironclads lying there so calm and peaceful, could, within a few short miles of us, be shining on the once beautiful city of Alexandria, now so ruthlessly shattered and destroyed by the terrible broadsides of those leviathan ships and the fanatic hordes let loose from its own prison walls.

The heavens and the sea were quiet and at peace; but in the land before us the passions of men had been let loose to destroy, not only the works, but the lives of their fellow-men.

As the fiery sun sank in the west, at once darkness began to close around, for here twilight is unknown. We were informed that the disembarkation would not take place till the next day. Anchor was cast close under the bows of H.M. torpedo ship "Hecla," a lovely vessel to the eye; but, as a sailor, to whom I was eulogising her beauty, said, "a veritable devil of the ocean." There was not much sleep that night, for everyone was anxious to be on shore; more especially as we knew that a regiment or two were already landed and eagerly looking for help. The longest night, however, comes to an end, and at the first streak of day we sailed alongside one of the many wharfs, and in a short half-hour we stood for the first time on Egyptian soil.

Arms were piled on the stone-laid quay, and we had a busy hour or two getting the heavy guns, carts, horses, &c., removed to *terra firma*. When this work was completed we fell into our ranks, and each man was served out with 70 rounds of ammunition, which caused a feeling to come over us that at last we were to be of use, even though it were but as targets. We tramped off through a few of the narrowest and most miserable-looking streets that ever it was my fortune to see. High houses, built without any semblance of regularity, small dingy holes for windows, flat roofs, almost closing in at the top, and leaving only a ragged strip of blue sky above. Paved with natural mother earth, worn into broad, deep holes here and there, such was the appearance of the native part of Alexandria.

Ere we had gone many hundred yards we came to a long and broad street, named Rue La-Ban. In it the houses were more substantial and European-looking, excepting that the roofs were all flat. Large shops of various kinds we passed, but all deserted and looted. There scarcely seemed to be any population left. Now and again a blue-gowned, white-turbaned Egyptian would peep round a corner with gaping mouth, as the hated Christians strode by; but they were few and far between.

Leaving this street, we emerged on to the Grand Square, once the handsomest part of the town, but now a mass of ruins, for the whole of the noble buildings surrounding it had been hurled to the ground. Costly furniture lay broken and smashed among heaps of stones and rubbish; merchandise of every description was scattered about. The half-burned contents of large warehouses were still smouldering in ashes. The demon of mischief had been madly revelling, and spreading devastation on all sides, for, as we marched on through what I may call the west end of Alexandria, the destruction to houses and property was indescribable. Here were standing the bare blackened walls of what had once been stately mansions, their whole interior destroyed by reckless incendiarism. Others again were intact so far as outward appearance went, but the street or grounds in front of them were strewn with furniture, massive looking glasses, wardrobes, pianos; whole libraries of finely-bound books lay smashed, torn, trampled, and utterly destroyed. Sometimes it seemed as if a less destructive band had entered, for only part of the furnishings were thrown out and lying undamaged around. As we picked our way through this ruinous scene, I heard several of my comrades remark, "What a g'orious chance of furnishing a house in elaborate and princely style, and all for nothing," as the owners had fled, preferring their lives to their worldly goods. About an hour's tramp brought us to the "Rossetta Gate," where we pitched our camp beside the 38th Regiment, who were glad to see us, for the enemy, under their leader Arabi, were not far off, and the troops to oppose them were as yet few.

On the following day the 38th left to proceed nearer to the enemy's lines, leaving us to guard the outer boundary of the town till we were relieved by the next batch of reinforcements.

I was extremely anxious to get a stroll through the ruined city before our departure, and, seizing the first available opportunity, four companions and I set out. We directed our steps towards Ras-el-Tin Palace, a splendid residence overlooking the Mediterranean. Its proximity to the Egyptian batteries had brought it partly under the fire of the war-ships, and it had suffered accordingly, one end being almost entirely demolished. With only a cursory glance at this palace of the Khedive of Egypt, we passed on to the batteries below. Here it was that the force of the heavy shells, thrown from such guns as were on board the "Inflexible," could be best realised. Every gun was disabled in some way or another; some were thrown on their beam-ends, others struck about their ponderous carriages, the bars of which were bent and twisted as if they were pieces of tiny wire instead of massive bars of iron 12 inches broad and 3 inches thick; and yet they were bent, not broadways, but edgeways, which may give the reader an idea of the tremendous blows they had received. It was evident that the fire from the ships had been well directed, for the whole of the batteries were virtually destroyed. We had not time to go further in search of destruction, so we hied back to our quarters again.

CHAPTER V.

AT RAMLEH : OUT-POST DUTY AND RECONNOITRING.

FOR two days we remained at Alexandria, and on the third day reinforcements arrived. Immediately we packed up our baggage, and marched off to Ramleh, a lovely country, thickly set with trees and gentlemen's residences ; and, about five miles from Alexandria, where we pitched our camp, this time on the brow of a sand hill close to the coast, and set to work to build forts for protection in case of an attack.

The enemy was not more than four miles in front, as from our camping-ground the outline of their rapidly-increasing earthworks at Kafr-el-Dowar could be faintly seen.

On the sea, about three miles off, lay a man-of-war, and every day her shells tore through the air high above our heads, speeding on their way to annoy and prevent the Egyptians from building their defences in peace.

Now we had to undertake that dreariest of all duties connected with war, viz., out-post duty, and that too in the very teeth of the enemy. It took about 150 men to form our section's out-posts every night, and the third time it came to my turn proved to be a lively night. The two previous nights were quiet, and I had been fortunate in being posted with a few men on the top of some of the numerous villas. There the worst part of the non-commissioned officer's work was to keep his men from romping about the houses, thumping on the pianos, and searching for the wine cellar, which, when they found, they did their best to make away with its contents.

But this night I was placed, with six men under my charge, on the side of a belt of trees in front of the line of sentries. Between this wood and the main body of the picket was a sandy plain about 400 yards wide, while in front of it extended a tract of level green fields, which, from our position (by the aid of an occasional flash of the electric light from our naval sentry in the bay), could be seen for a long way. Our duty was to watch, and if we saw any sign of living men in front, retire back on the main body with the intelligence. Two men were continually on the look-out, while the remainder of us reclined amongst the trees. I suppose it might have been about midnight when, without the least warning, a sharp volley of musketry rang from the picket behind us, and the bullets crashed against the tree-tops over our head.

The readers must keep in mind that this was our first angry shot, and they must bear with us patiently if we showed a little trepidation.

Another and another volley followed, and now the yells of the Arabs were heard between us and the pickets. Crossing to the edge of the trees, we saw a large body of horsemen galloping madly hither and thither, within 100 yards of us. They were evidently as much surprised and frightened as we were, for they were calling loudly, "Allah! Allah!" the name of their god. We crawled close to the fence skirting the wood, and, with beating hearts, waited for the crisis. Again the rifles of the picket spoke, but the trees above got most of the bullets. We had our rifles loaded, and ammunition ready for action, but I gave instructions not to fire, as we did not want those wild Bedouins to know our whereabouts, and very soon they galloped away to the left, firing a retaliating shot occasionally ere they swept out of sight.

For about a quarter of an hour we kept our place, the musketry still going on; but, instead of the ringing volleys, it was now a dropping, independent fire. A short consultation was held, which resulted in the decision being arrived at to make our way back to where the main body of the picket lay. But this was rendered a dangerous task, as only the officer who placed us here knew our position, and, in the excitement now raised, the very moment we appeared in sight in all probability meant a dozen bullets flying at us from the rifles of our own comrades. We had, therefore, to be very cautious in retracing our steps, and stealthily we stole along, keeping the shadow of the wood until we reached the back-grounds of a gentleman's residence. Up the side of the high garden wall we crept in perfect silence, and now only 200 yards intervened between us and the place where we left the main body, but that intervening space was open, level sand. The moment we emerged forth upon it, the quick eye of the sentries might detect us, and a bullet would, in all likelihood, be our first challenge. I, being in charge of the party, took upon myself the risk of this, and, making my way on hands and knees, every now and then halting and taking a good survey, I reached the station house on the railway line where the picket had been; but now they were gone. Thinking I must have got mixed up somehow or other in my latitude, I made a careful examination around and satisfied myself that it was the same place where we had left our comrades. I went back to my men with this intelligence, and, as the firing was still going

Out-post Duty and Reconnoitring. 39

smartly on about a mile from us and more in the direction of the camp, we looked on the blackest side of the picture, and at once jumped to the conclusion that the out-posts were all driven in, leaving us behind. This did not prove a very pleasant reflection, for, if such were the case, there seemed little hope that we could force our way through the enemy to our own lines.

Though a good deal scared, we resolved to do our best, and on we came to the station house with the intention of waiting under cover till the firing had somewhat subsided. A quarter of an hour had barely passed when the sound of advancing footsteps were heard coming along the railway line. Soon a black moving mass appeared, whether friend or foe we knew not. It would never do to let this advancing band close up before we ascertained who or what they were, and I gave my men hasty instructions to run at their greatest speed for a thick, extensive grove of trees some 200 yards away, in case of an adverse reply. I raised my voice, and, with apparent boldness, shouted, "Who comes there?" With what thankfulness we heard the ringing reply, "friend!" in the well-known tones of the officer commanding the pickets. The first words he addressed to me on his arrival were, "Where have you been?" I explained to him where I was posted, and what had occurred. He then made inquiry whether any of my men were hurt, and, receiving a reply in the negative, sent for the officer who had placed us there, and took him severely to task for exposing us in such a dangerous position where we could see nothing but the plain in front, while all the time the enemy could come on us by following the wood which stretched almost to their trenches. The danger from our own sentries was also great, as they were watching the outskirts of the wood, and being unaware of our presence in it, the least movement among the trees would have been taken for a movement of the enemy. During that night no more men were placed where we had been ; and I was not again on out-post at that part of the line.

It turned out, from information received from prisoners who were captured, that the night's diversion had been caused by a party of mounted Bedouins in search of plunder, and they, unconscious of the close proximity of the pickets, had themselves been plundered of the lives of about a dozen of their number.

Such a beginning as the above soon hardens the soldier to lonely out-posts, for, had the same sort of thing happened to the same party a few weeks after, what a smash we would have made among those Bedouins from behind the fence which skirted that wood.

Some days after this a rumour got abroad in the camp that the Arabs were vacating their earthworks at Kafr-el-Dowar, and, to prove the truth of this rumour, General Sir A. Allison, then in command, ordered a reconnaissance in some force to be made in that direction.

About 4 p.m. on the 6th August, 1882, four companies of our regiment, the 2nd D.C.L.I., and the same number of the South Stafford Regiment, started off by the banks of the Mahoudied Canal, accompanied by about 50 men of the Mounted Infantry. At the same time the 60th Rifles moved along the opposite bank ; while away further to the right an armour-clad train, conveying the Naval Brigade and a battalion of Marines, steamed slowly along the railway line.

Both the railway and the canal, though a good distance apart, run right through the enemy's fortifications.

For two miles we tramped on without molestation.

Then several heavy puffs of white smoke rose in the clear air about one mile in front, followed in a few seconds by the "whiz" of advancing shells. Those dire missiles of war came on with a rushing sound, changing their tune as they approached to a tearing roar, rending the very air in their mad career. This was our first acquaintance with those murderous customers, and it was with a feeling of something like—I will not be far wrong if I say fear—that we waited breathlessly for them to reach their destination, and it was with thankfulness that we heard one after another crash into the earth around without doing any damage. Very few of them exploded, which was fortunate for us. This, my first experience of shells, draws from me the opinion that there are few, if any, men who can stand in cool blood and hear the swishing rush of those lumps of metal as they fly towards them, for the first time, without being sensible of a feeling of trepidation creeping over them.

One has only to glance round the faces, and in the quivering lips and firm-set teeth the tension on the nerves can be distinctly traced. The eye also, that tell-tale of all emotions, gazes forward with a peculiar troubled expression in its glassy depths, which nothing but inward dread compels it to assume.

Not that there was any more visible sign of what was passing within. No, we were too British for that, and, even amid the birring of the shells, an occasional laugh would break out at some one who ducked his head uncommonly low as they passed over, but it was not the laugh of merriment : its hollow ring plainly said it was forced.

Deploying into a thin skirmishing line, we continued our advance, shell after shell roaring past, I may say, almost harmlessly, for not one in our regiment was hit, and our dread of them was fast wearing off.

The Naval Brigade was manfully returning the compliment from their guns on the train, while the quick rattle of musketry told us that the gallant Marines were already in action. From a grove of palm trees in front of them the white smoke was rising in incessant puffs, and they were vigorously replying.

Now it was our turn. A sharp fusilade whistled about us, also from a clump of palm or fig trees some 900 yards off, and we opened fire in reply. Directly our rifles spoke, the fast-fading sensation of nervousness vanished, and in its place came a fierce desire to push on, and close with the enemy. But they would not wait, and ten minutes sufficed to send them swarming back to their trenches, all with the exception of one, who remained up a tree standing by itself further off than the rest. He sat close be'ow the heavy clump of branches on the half-grown palm tree, and from this point of vantage he peppered away at us. Regularly his rifle flashed, and the solitary bullet whistled amongst us with an annoying sound. A lieutenant and one man of the Mounted Infantry fell dead, supposed from this man's rifle. Many a shot was directed at him, but he seemed to bear a charmed life. Had we only known the exact distance, he might not have lived so long. I believe 100 bullets were fired at him before he fell from his perch, which he eventually did. People who are reading this will be apt to say, "what bad shots," but let me tell them that several renowned marksmen emptied their rifles different times at this "man in the tree." He was a long way off, and there was no means of gauging the exact distance, for the fields behind and in front of him were cultivated, and no sign of the

Out-post Duty and Reconnoitring.

striking bullets could be detected: besides, he looked little bigger than a child.

The fighting was over as far as we were concerned; not so with the Marines: they had encountered a stronger and more determined body, and, before they succeeded in making the Egyptians run for their forts, they had lost about thirty men killed and wounded. We had clearly proved that the enemy had not as yet vacated their position, for, on the top of the earthworks in front, they clustered in thousands.

Our object was however gained, and the order came to retire. The Arabs claimed this as a victory, and the sullen boom of their cannon and the noisy shells followed us till we were completely out of range.

Reinforcements were daily pouring in, and, in little more than a week, the ground for over a mile square was a scattered mass of white tents. Lord Wolseley had also arrived to guide the operations, and every day we expected the order to march on Kafr-el-Dowar; but, judge of our surprise when at mid-day, on the 18th August, the command ran swiftly through the spreading camp, "pack up at once and be ready to go on board ship at Alexandria."

CHAPTER VI.

EN ROUTE FOR ISHMAILIA: ARRIVAL AT ISHMAILIA.

N the afternoon of the 18th August there was nothing but bustle in the camp. A surburban railway, some five miles in length, connected Ramleh with Alexandria, and thither we carried our baggage for conveyance to the latter place. Each regiment in succession sent off their camp equipment; but, before it came to our turn, darkness had set in, and work was stopped for the night. A party of twenty men under charge of a sergeant and myself (then a corporal) were detailed to look after the regiment's belongings, and come on with it in the early morning.

The battalion had marched to Alexandria to take up their quarters on board H.M. troopship "Euphrates."

Before daylight we were hard at work loading the trucks, and sunrise saw us whirling down the line seated on the top of high piles of tents, blankets, &c., of which the trucks had been laden. On arrival at the station, though little more than a fortnight had passed since we left it, we saw that a vast change had taken place. The people, reassured by the appearance of the ever-increasing British troops, had largely found their way back to their occupations, for the station, instead of its then deserted appearance, now showed no indication that the country was in the throes of war, except the unusual number of soldiers bustling about. Natives' carts were conveying our goods to the ship; but they were coming very slow, and a message came from the colonel to hurry up, as the ship was only waiting to get us on board ere she sped on her way. The baggage of other regiments that had arrived on the preceding day was still lying at the station, and a rivalry set in between the various corps to get away first. Parties of men patrolled the streets in the vicinity, and, as the long narrow Egyptian carts made their appearance, they were pounced upon, and, whichever regiment got possession, the driver had to go with them whether he was willing or not: it was first come first served. We had obtained a good few carts in this manner, when, I suppose, it came to be feeding time for man and horse; at anyrate, for about an hour and a half no carts were to be got.

To while away the time, I, accompanied by the sergeant in charge and several non-commissioned officers of the other regiments, strolled into a refreshment-room near by. What a sight met us: the place was packed with soldiers clamouring to be supplied with drink. The poor Greek in charge was totally unable to cope with the demand, and evidently had not made preparations for such visitors as soldiers fresh from the first taste of war. The shelves all round his shop were filled with bottles, and these were gradually disappearing, while round the counter the commotion was so great that the fellow lost his head entirely. On seeing us come in, he called vehemently in some foreign language, and pointed to his fast-emptying shelves. We did our best to stem this reckless tide of wholesale robbery, not so much for the sake of the man's losses, but more with the object of keeping the men sober and fit for work when the carts again begun to arrive.

I was the proud possessor of two shillings, and I bought a bottle of what the seller termed "best con-ē-ak," but it was vile stuff. We went round behind a pile of baggage, and soon demolished the contents of the bottle, but oh! it was fiery. I think it must have been for drinking sake that such a raid was made on the greedy Greek's shop: it could not have been for love of the liquor. Sheer devilment possessed them, and the fact that he sold no biscuits or food of any sort exasperated the hungry soldiers, for few of them had tasted food that day. Not one got tipsy, however, which was a proof that they were not consuming all they took.

Glad were we when the carts began to rattle on the streets, and a squad was sent out to waylay them, and bring them in, willing or not. For the next two hours all was hurry, and at last we despatched the last load. Forming up the meagre remains of the party (the majority of which had been sent on as escort to the different carts, and a number had not returned), we marched off, and with not a litt'e difficulty found our way to the ship's side. We expected a good blowing-up from the colonel for being so long in arriving, but evidently some one had informed him of our difficulty in getting the means of transport, for he congratulated both the sergeant and me on sending everything to the ship's side correctly, considering the odds we had to contend against.

Taking advantage of his good humour, we gave him a gentle hint that it was now four o'clock, and no food of any kind had passed our lips since the previous night. The whole party belonged to one company, and our captain, overhearing the remarks, at once came forward and made inquiries himself. "That will never do, my boys," says he. "You must be fed, and if I can do anything you will be fed, and that properly. Come away down with me to the steward's room, and we will see

what he can do for you." Down the stairs we went in
high glee, as a hungry man must be when joints of beef
and ham rise in front of him. Away went the captain in
search of the steward, and gave him instructions to give
us a substantial dinner at his (the captain's) expense.
Right well did the steward obey the order, for he packed us
with cold beef, ham, fowls, &c., and finished us off with
two pints of beer each, and a lump of bread and cheese.
Occasionally the captain looked in, and asked us how we
were faring. He was of the right sort, and the company
missed him sorely after the battle of Kassassin (he being
wounded, and sent home from there.)

With well-filled stomachs and brightened spirits, the
latter by the effects of beer, we sailied to the troop-
deck to rejoin our comrades and look out for our
quarters. I did not come on deck till it was nearly dark,
and by that time we had left the harbour, and were steaming slowly along the coast side in company with some half-
dozen large steamers that had been hired and fitted up to
convey troops. About the same number of men-of-war
were escorting us on the way.

We were not aware where our destination was—
rumour said Aboukir Bay, and in that belief we retired to
our hammocks for the night. In the morning, when I went
on deck, land was not in sight, but a sailor told me that
we were nearing Port Said. About 10 a.m., a low-lying
coast appeared ahead, and in a short time we slowed up
at the mouth of the Suez Canal, and had a look at the
grimy hovels of the dirty-looking town of Port Said. A
motley group of Arabs hung about the piers, and, judging
from their looks and general appearance, a more rascally
set I never saw. We had no wish to land, neither did we
get the chance ; for, after a deal of flag-signalling between

the various ships, an ironclad came steaming up, and took up a position close to a French war ship which was lying near the entrance to the canal in a menacing sort of way. Her topmasts were lowered, her guns run out, as if she was prepared to bar our onward way. The British ironclad followed her example, for, as she swung into position, down came her topmasts, and her guns were run out ready for action. Whether it was that the French objected to us going down the canal (hence this demonstration) I know not; but, if such had been their intention, they were baulked.

A gunboat led the way into the canal, followed by the "Euphrates," steered by her own captain, as not a pilot could be got. All that day we steamed slowly down this narrow channel of water with its almost unbroken line of sand banks, and sandy wastes behind, on which the fierce sun glared with blistering heat. When darkness set in, the engines stopped to wait till the morning light. About twenty men had to climb the rigging on to a platform erected on the mast at the cross-yards to watch and ward over our safety for the night. Nothing happened to disturb us, and long before I was awake the ship was gliding on.

Late in the afternoon we steamed into the broad lake of Tismah, on the right of which lay the town of Ishmailia, a much more prepossessing place than Port Said. Besides the Arab houses, there were a few European buildings of modern style situated among palm and other trees, which gave a pleasant green-like look to this eastern village, which proved refreshing after the miles of continuous sand we had passed.

Barges were soon alongside, and the work of disembarkation commenced. About this time the captain from the bridge had been giving some orders to a number of men, who were engaged throwing loose hay from the ship on to the barge below. What the orders were I did not catch, but they evidently gave amusement to the men, for several of them indulged in a half-smothered laugh. This was too much for the captain, as he had been in a rage the whole day (having run the ship aground in the morning), and now he seized the opportunity of venting his wrath on those unfortunate smilers. He ordered four of them to be brought to the quarter-deck, and I, being near by, was told to accompany them. The punishment meted out was for them to stand strictly at " attention " without a move until he should see fit to allow them to go. My task, I believe, was as bad as theirs, for I had to watch and report to the captain the first man that moved even so much as his little finger ; and, for a short time, the captain took note that I performed my part; if I did not, I was told that I had to fall-in and do my turn at " attention." For about half an hour we kept our places. Fortunately, the captain had to attend to other duties now and again, and, signalling by looks, I made the men understand when to move and when not to.

All our comrades had left the ship except five men, who were left behind to bring the remainder of the baggage, and I received orders to bring them and all the belongings of the regiment with me by the next barge. The captain, after getting his revenge partly assuaged by seeing those four men standing like sticks on the quarter-deck, now came up, took down their names, and writing out a formidable charge, bade me hand it and the men over to the colonel (as prisoners) when I joined the regiment. This was the second occasion on which I was left to bring up the rear of the regiment. By this time it was quite dark, and no sign of the barge coming to take us away, and, as the ship had to sail in the early morning, two boats were lowered : one was loaded with the left equipment, and into the other the ten of us went. The sailors manned the oars and rowed to Her Majesty's gunboat " Falcon," lying near by, where we were stowed away for the night. Here we passed a few comfortable hours, huddled up among the piles of blankets we had brought with us.

Long before daylight, I was awakened by a noise on board, and, on looking up, I saw the sailors crowding round a big tub-full of steaming coffee, each dipping a jug in turn for their morning drink. We were invited to join them, and you may be sure we did so, for the morning was bitterly cold, making the hot coffee delicious. When the sun rose, an order was passed to the crew that five minutes would be allowed for bathing. This order created quite a scene : off went Jack Tar's clothes, and in a few seconds their nude figures were flying from deck, mast, and spar into the water below. Our taste at that early hour was not so aquatic as Jack's, and we did not join in the swim, but waited patiently till it was over, when we were treated to a good breakfast. Before it was devoured, the barge was alongside waiting. Our baggage was thrown in, and, scrambling over the ship's side, we bade good-bye to the crew of H.M. gunboat " Falcon." They had supplied us all with pieces of tobacco to smoke on the march, which proved a great comfort. For myself, I was presented with a roll weighing about 1½ pounds, closely tied round with " tarry tow," and the bulk was such that I could not carry it in my pocket, and afterwards, when our accoutrements had to be left behind, I hung it on the brass hook at the side of my coat, where it became almost company property, for, when I slept, those who were in want of a smoke stealthily cut off a pipeful as long as it lasted.

About mid-day we rejoined the regiment, and I delivered the document against my prisoners handed to me by the captain of the " Euphrates ; " but the colonel sent them off to their companies without a word, and they never afterwards heard about it. The camp was in a beautiful grove of palm trees, with a clear, splashing fountain in the centre, and I was praising the surroundings, when a comrade said to me : " If you had been here last night, you would have thought it different." This prompted me to enquire, and I was told that a false alarm had occurred. It appeared that, about the dead of night, one of the outlying sentries had fired a few shots at an imaginary enemy. The regiment had sprung up in haste ; in fact too much haste, for, in the black darkness under the shadow of the trees, there had been a lively five minutes. Rifles could not be found ; men scrambled over each other in their eager search. To make matters worse, a number of men were partly undressed, and several of them had on white cotton shirts, and (as my companion told me) they were taken for Arabs, and, as such, they were treated rather roughly. I was glad I was not in it, for a proper night surprise is one of the most fearsome things that can befall a regiment or army in time of war. I have experienced one or two of those alarms ; but, somehow or other, directly on waking up I knew at once where I was and what were my surroundings. Some men take longer time than others to bring their proper senses into working order, and those are the men who rush about, only half awake—not only frightened themselves, but frightening others, thereby bringing disgrace on their regiments. My verdict is : give me fifty battles before one of those horrible night alarms.

The regiment was not destined to stay for another night in this place, as the order came to march.

Loading our tents, &c., on carts and pack-mules, we set out across a sandy plain, and, on the side of a sandy hill, some three miles from Ishmailia, we pitched our camp, and remained there for two days acting as an advanced guard to protect the landing of the main body of the British army preparatory to their attack on Tel-el-Kebir.

CHAPTER VII.

FIGHT AT EL-MAGFAR: SCENE IN A MELON FIELD.

AT about five a.m. on the morning of the 25th August, 1882, while we were in the act of removing our camp a mile or two further from Ishmailia, the 19th Hussars and two batteries of Royal Marine Artillery passed us on their way (in soldier's parlance) to the "front." We gave them an encouraging cheer as they filed on, and continued the work of making our tents inhabitable. About nine a.m. the bugle sounded for breakfast, and there was a rush for the much-needed meal. I was in my tent, along with a number of comrades, when a boiling-hot kettleful of coffee was carried in and distributed in equal shares into each man's canteen. Most of us were in our shirt sleeves squatting on the sand, and devouring hard regulation biscuits, waiting for the coffee to cool, when the bugles rang out the "Assembly." That call is answered by a sharp turn-out, even in barracks; but, with the enemy in the near vicinity, it means simply a maddening charge. Coats, arms, accoutrements, &c., were thrown on in wild confusion, canteens of coffee upset in the *melee* for first on parade. In a space of time almost incredible to a non-military man, we were dashing from the tents and forming in the ranks, eagerly scanning the country around for a sight of the foe; but no: we had to go to them. Fours-right, quick march! came the sharply-uttered command, and away we tramped through the soft sand, sinking several inches at every step. We knew from the stern looks of our respected commander, and his hurried whispering to the other officers, that some new development of the enemy had taken place which required our immediate attention. The sun was beating down on us with a savage heat, as mile after mile we covered at a rapid rate, the colonel leading the way on horseback and occasionally riding along the companies, cheering them on to even greater speed.

This was a "forced march," and only those who have toiled in the arid deserts of the East under a broiling sun, suffering from that worst of all wants, water, can realise its terrible nature. Two hours had scarcely elapsed ere the sullen roar of the cannons was heard in front, telling us that the troops who passed in the early morning had been checked in their way, and were now fighting their first battle with the Egyptian army. On we went, every man at his best, and, as the saying is, "the weakest going to the wall;" for now men could be seen staggering along as though intoxicated, until they finally sunk on the sand utterly exhausted. We had no time to help; they looked up to us with piteous faces as we trod on, with set teeth and knitted brows, for our powers of endurance were fading fast, and we knew not the moment we would have to succumb. Our colonel evidently came to the conclusion that a short halt was necessary, if he wanted to take the major part of his men to the journey's end. Just as we were crossing a railway embankment, we got this respite. Throwing ourselves down on the hot sand, we lay with the cannons' loud roar in our ears, and about two miles of our recent track in view, thickly dotted with the scarlet coats of some 200 of our comrades, a few struggling on after us, but the majority lying where they had fallen. It was a dangerous game we were playing, for, had the Arabs got scent of those exhausted men, their fate was sealed.

Time was precious, and we were soon on the move; but the hardest part of our march was over. The demon "thirst" was, however, twining his fangs tighter and tighter, and not a drop of water to be had. Rounding the end of a ridge of sand hills, we went right into a green field. With a cry of delight the regiment welcomed the order to "Fall-out," for it was a melon field. The ripe, heavy melons were there in hundreds, and for about three minutes the scene was amusing and ludicrous Our gray-haired colonel sat on his horse busily eating a melon, which some one had handed up to him. All around him scarlet coats and big green leaves blended in harmonious mixture. Then, thinking we had got enough, he gave the order to "Fall-in," but only those near heard the command, as most of us were so intently engaged slicing and eating the delicious fruit that all else was forgotten.

For myself, I can say that neither before nor since has a melon had the same refreshing taste as they had on that day.

But now, as if to punish us for our thieving propensities, a shell from one of the enemy's guns tore the air overhead, and exploded with a loud report in our midst. Looking in the direction from which it came, we saw that we were in full view of their batteries, and they did not forget us. Shell after shell whistled around us, and, as they exploded, their jagged fragments flew in all directions. Mingling with the din of this iron shower came the cries of pain as body and limb were torn and mangled by those horrid splinters.

Quickly we re-formed and doubled from the field, carrying our wounded comrades with us, and also a plentiful supply of melons, which, even in the hands of wounded men, were firmly grasped. We made our way across an open plain in rear of our own batteries, and there the sight was sufficient to send the blood leaping through the veins with excitement and admiration. Those brave fellows were stripped to their shirts and trousers, sleeves rolled up, the perspiration streaming from their faces as they loaded and fired like " devils let loose." Before a gun had ceased to rebound from the concussion of firing, half-a-dozen hands were on the wheel putting it in position again. They were fighting against fearful odds ; it was a case of 40 cannon to 10, but there was no flinching. The shells crashed around that little band, but they heeded them not. As my company was passing one of the batteries, I observed a tall artilleryman directing his eye along his gun, apparently taking careful aim. While so doing, his head was literally blown to pieces ; but, ere his lifeless body had reached the ground, another was in his place, and in a twinkling an angry report rang from the muzzle as if bidding defiance to the numerous foe.

We were not long before we gained the shelter of another bank of sandy hills, and there lay for the rest of the day ready to repel an attack on that noble band of gunners, if such were made. An occasional shell came tearing amongst us, but did no damage till one of those daring fellows, "war correspondents," came galloping up on horseback and dismounted on the higher ground in front. Throwing the reins over his arm, he sat down on a camp-stool, produced his note-book, and set to work. The enemy, no doubt eyeing him through their field-glasses, and probably thinking he was devising a plan for their annihilation, poured a perfect torrent of shot and shell about his "devoted head." But he was made of the real stuff; for he wrote on. Sometimes he was hid from our view in a cloud of sand, raised by a shell falling within a few yards of him. As it cleared away, he was seen to shake the remnants of it from his note-book and continue his task. It eventually got too hot for his charger, for it plunged and reared to such an extent that the brave writer had to remount and seek a more safe retreat. Glad were we when he left, for the shells meant for him came dancing amongst us in a rather unpleasant manner.

During the evening we could see vast masses of reinforcements moving towards us over the wide plain that stretched behind, and, as the first of them came up (which proved to be another battery of artillery), the shells went high over our heads to meet and give them a taste of what was in store when they came closer. Darkness put a stop to this contest without a gain on either side, and, under the cloud of night, we silently advanced over the soft sand to the foot of the long sloping ground within 600 yards of the top, on which stood the Egyptian batteries. Forming into a thin line, we halted and lay down for the night. Our general and staff passed along on foot, stopping at about every twelve paces, and, in low and subdued tones, they informed us that the safety of the whole army was in our keeping. Whether the general used the same words to convey his meaning at all parts of the line I know not; but I remember well what he said at the place where I lay. It was this: "Men, you have the place of honour; the safety of your comrades, and the glory of your country in your keeping; you must stand or fall where you now are, even though the whole army of Egypt come against you." With this assurance he left us to spend our weary night in the desert.

 Pickets were posted a short distance in front to give the alarm in case of an attack, and, though hungry, I was soon in a sound sleep. On awakening, I sat up and looked around: all was quiet and still. The colour-sergeant of my company lay near, and, on observing me staring about, he asked if I was looking for food. I told him I was half-famished with hunger. "Oh, if that is all," said he, "we will soon cure you, for during the time you were sleeping a party of men went round distributing rations of tinned beef, biscuits, and water, and I, not being willing to spoil your sleep, kept your share." With that he put his hand round to his haversack which hung on his back, and giving vent to an oath, said, "some devil has stolen it." Sure enough there was no food in the haversack; it had been taken out while he had been asleep. Some of our comrades near by, overhearing the conversation, got up a collection of left fragments, and, after all, I had a fair and much-needed supper; for, barring the melons, I had eaten nothing since the previous night.

CHAPTER VIII.

WITH THE ADVANCED GUARD TO KASSASSIN.

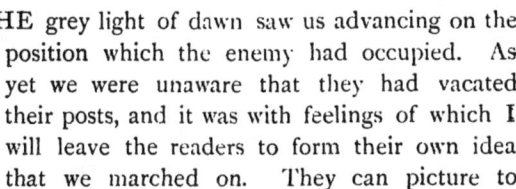HE grey light of dawn saw us advancing on the position which the enemy had occupied. As yet we were unaware that they had vacated their posts, and it was with feelings of which I will leave the readers to form their own idea that we marched on. They can picture to themselves a front line of skirmishers moving steadily forward towards a long ridge of gradually-sloping sand hills, on the summit of which could be seen the earthworks from where the guns of the enemy had poured such a deadly shower on the preceding day. Every moment we expected them to blaze out again in all their fury, accompanied, as they would be, by the still more deadly rattle of musketry, for by this time we were within range of that weapon. I can assure you that hearts beat fast with suppressed excitement. It is in such positions as this that the bravery of the British soldier shines above all others. In the roar of battle it is quite different, for then the blood is up; but this slow and steady march, into what we imagined to be the very jaws of death, puts an indescribable tension on even a strong nerve.

When within about 300 yards the remark passed freely along the ranks, " Won't we catch it when they do wake up ! " but no, all was silent, and a halt was ordered. An officer was seen to gallop to the brow of the hill without molestation, and then we knew the foe had fled. Instantly there was a commotion among the staff surrounding Lord

Wolseley: mounted officers galloped hither and thither with new instructions to the various corps. Up dashed two batteries of Royal Horse Artillery, the 19th Hussars, and about 50 Mounted Infantry. They swept majestically past us in all the pride of military glory, bent on the tracks of the flying enemy. Our regiment and another got orders to continue our position as advanced guard and follow on, while the main body were marched to the bank of a water canal, about a mile and a half to the right, and there encamped.

During the forenoon march, I saw, for the first time, that deceptive and tantalising phenomenon, " the mirage " —tantalising for this reason, that it is only to be seen when the sun glares down on the hot sands of the desert where water is in great demand, and none to be got; and yet in front of us only a little way lay imitation lakes of tempting silvery water, with imaginary trees and shrubs dotted over the glassy surface. It was all so real-like that one could almost be certain he would in a few minutes be splashing amongst the cool delicious element. But no : it was that delusion known to desert travellers as the mirage, for all around us there was nothing but sand.

Scarcely an hour had passed ere the loud boom of cannon broke on our ears, mingled with the ringing report of the Martini-Henry. The Royal Horse and Mounted Infantry had overtaken the Egyptians, and were paying them back for the almost total extinction of the brave band of gunners who so nobly upheld the honour of Britain, and proved a match for them on the previous day. Water-carts were following in our rear, and they were occasionally driven up to supply us with the precious beverage, to which a barrel of Highland whisky could not have been compared (in our position) to one single cupful.

About 10 a.m. we sighted the deserted camp of the enemy; they had been shelled out. Our route leading us close by it, the colonel allowed us to "fall-out" for a brief space. We made good use of our time, for, prompted by a feeling of curiosity, we ransacked every tent, and I will not say but that a few of the smaller valuables followed their owners in the pockets of the British soldier. There was a great difference in their fighting equipment from ours. Here we stood with only what was on our backs—not even a greatcoat to protect us from the bitterly cold August mornings. A few straps buckled round us, a haversack with a day's rations in it, and 130 rounds of ammunition, completed our store. Those fellows had evidently been living in the land of plenty: provisions were scattered about in galore, clothing of every description, from the richly-embroidered garb of the pasha to the white uniforms of the rank and file. Women's garments were also plentiful, showing that those warriors had their lady-loves with them. About a mile ahead was the railway station of Mahsameh, and from the tents to it the whole way bore the ghastly traces of the recent conflict. Dead, dying, and wounded lay in hundreds. We were by no means hard-hearted when the blood was cool, and we carried a number of those disabled men into the shade of the station house and the trucks or carriages that stood on the line. The canal here came close to, and ran almost parallel with, the railway track, and along its banks lay the dead and dying Egyptians, shot down by the mounted infantry while endeavouring to escape.

A sergeant of our regiment, who was attached to the mounted infantry, here gained a medal for distinguished bravery in the field. He was a real rollicking son of the Emerald Isle, named Michael, or, as we called him, Mike O'Reardon. When the Egyptians were flying to the last train which was to convey them off, he dashed away from his troop and plunged through the seething mass. His quick eye had detected that the couplings of the second carriage were slack, and he made for it. Springing from his horse he undid them, and the engine steamed off, leaving our gallant Mike the capturer of about twenty trucks and carriages (some of them loaded with provisions and ammunition) and some 300 prisoners. Of course, it was done in a moment, for his troop was not far behind, and the Egyptians were so taken by surprise, that, before they got time to think of sending Mike to his long home, the mounted infantry thundered in amongst them. He was presented with his medal by the Queen's own hand some time after.

We were restricted from drinking from the canal within a distance of 300 yards, as it was considered by the medical men who accompanied us to be dangerous to our health, owing to the numerous dead bodies in it and on its banks; but many a drink was stolen, for all that, within this quarantine limit. A desultory musketry skirmish was still going on a few miles ahead, but the artillery had relinquished the chase, and were resting near by. We expected to remain here a day or two, and set to work to rig up some sort of awning to protect us from the blazing sun. Sticks and stalks of Indian corn tied together for strength were stuck in the ground. Jackets were stripped off, fastened together, and stretched over those improvised uprights with a good deal of ingenuity, for necessity is the mother of invention. We were not destined to have a long stay. A sagacious head was directing our operations, and five p.m. saw us on the way to take possession of, and retain, a lock-bridge which crossed the canal at Kassassin. This was a wise thought, for on its waters depended the existence of the whole army. Had the enemy got time to destroy the bridge, or turn the water on to the adjoining land, which could easily have been done, a dire calamity would have befallen us all.

Just as darkness was enveloping the land, we arrived at this bridge and found it deserted, for, with the cavalry at their heels, the enemy had passed it in hot haste, and as yet they had not found courage to return. We were now cut off from all communication with the main body, and every precaution was taken against surprise. Out-posts were thrown out, and warned to be on the alert, while the remainder of us lay down in companies, fully armed and accoutred, with our legs slipped through the slings of our rifles, so that in case of a sudden surprise they would be more easily found in the dark. However, we were not disturbed, and morning broke clear and unclouded as usual, and perfect quietness reigned around, with no sign of either friend or foe. We had as much rations in our haversacks as formed a light breakfast, which was our last meal till noon on the third day. The next two days we lived on muddy water and fresh air. We had a few mules for carrying ammunition, and they were picketed between us and the canal. On the afternoon of the second day sentries had to be posted to prevent us stealing the beans with which they were fed, for at these times a drought seemed to take possession of us. Numbers wended their way past the feeding animals to the canal, and in spite of the watchful eye of the sentry, many a sudden dive of the hand was made into the mouth-bags, and a handful of beans was quickly transferred to the pockets. The third day, the 28th August, 1882, was a memorable one to the 1400 men who held the bridge, for on it was fought the first battle of Kassassin, culminating in the famous moonlight charge of the Heavy Dragoon Guards.

CHAPTER IX.

BATTLE OF KASSASSIN.

THE sun rose on the morning of the 28th August, 1882, and looked down on as strange a camp as I imagine British soldiers ever occupied. The absence of tents had drawn out all our resources of ingenuity in devising a canopy to protect us from old Sol's fierce rays. The green fields on the opposite banks of the canal supplied us partly with material. Every man built his own "shanty" according to his ideas of comfort. Generally speaking, our abodes were a long and narrow hole dug in the sand to a depth of from one to two feet, and bearing a gruesome resemblance to the six feet of earth man claims as his last resting-place. Here and there two or three had clubbed together, and the result was a more elaborate dwelling. Among the soft sand shovelled out were placed upright stakes, roofed over with leaves, shrubs, &c., in fact anything that would keep out the sun's glare. Some, not putting themselves to much trouble, had simply a few sticks driven in the ground and their well-worn jackets spread over them, and, when they lay down, hid their heads under this welcome shade. Others, following the more "civilised and prevalent custom"—be respectable outside, come what may of the inner—were to all outward appearance fully dressed; but over their heads floated the grey folds of their only regulation shirt. Such is human nature.

Battle of Kassassin.

We had been too hungry to sleep the sleep of the contented, and, after a broken night's rest, our first thought turned on the problem, "Are we to get any food to-day?" It may seem incredible to many, but it is nevertheless true, that a party of men were despatched along the banks of the canal to gather dirty brown biscuits, which in their haste the retreating enemy had thrown away in large quantities. The best of these were picked up and handed over to the quartermaster, who, in turn, distributed one between three men. Mouldy and dirty as they were, each man ate his square inch and longed for more. Clearly something must be done, as matters were getting serious. There was an Arab village about $1\frac{1}{2}$ miles off, on the opposite side of the canal, and we knew from experience that, in all likelihood, poultry would be there in abundance. The natives, however, hated the very sight of us, and had refused to sell; nothing would have pleased them better than to see us starve. The cry arose, "Let us go and take," but discipline has such a firm hold on the soldier that no one dared take the lead.

In the early forenoon an order was given for each company to prepare a party, and proceed to this village and bring back a supply of firewood. Firewood; what did we want with it? The very word seemed hollow mockery; we had nothing to cook. Somehow or other it got whispered about that once we were there we might as well bring something else. We set out on our quest, and it appeared to us as if our gallant general in command, Sir Gerald Graham, was following in the footsteps of Scotland's greatest hero, Sir William Wallace, when he said to his army, "I have brought you to the ring; dance according to your skill." At anyrate the fact of his sending us there we took to mean, "I have sent you

Battle of Kassassin. 67

where there is plenty; see that you do not let the opportunity slip." Perhaps our hungry state helped us to this conclusion. You may be sure we did not let it slip, for while the officers and sergeants and a few men were looking after the firewood, the remainder were busy catching cocks, hens, and chickens. The natives made little or no objection to this raid on their poultry; our uncouth appearance evidently frightened them, for a razor was a thing of the past. They were, however, paid for their losses afterwards. It was with joy that our comrades saw us return laden with the spoils of Egypt. We had several camp kettles, which formed part of the equipment of the regimental cooks, and these being supplemented by a few tin boxes, operations began. Fires were lit, fowls killed and plucked, and soon we were having a substantial repast. We also had an eye to the future, for the fowls that were not to be eaten at once were tied up by the legs to our accoutrement straps, rifles, &c., as convenient. By 1 p.m. the scene was one of animation. As our stomachs filled our spirits rose, and mingling with our hearty laughter came the cackling of hens and screeching of chicks as they tugged to get free.

Things had assumed a brighter aspect, when suddenly the stirring notes of the "assemble" broke on our ears. Instantly the scene changed; accoutrements were buckled hastily on, rifles snatched up, the tied-up poultry were released by a quick slash of our massive clasp knives which were hung round our necks by a strong cord, and served as knife, fork, and spoon combined. Away we dashed into our places in the ranks, and also away dashed the frightened fowls. We had barely time to form, when, under a cloud of dust about a mile off, and bearing straight for us at full gallop, came a large body of Egyptian cavalry.

Battle of Kassassin.

Wheeling into line we marched out to meet the foe. When some 800 yards intervened, we got the order to fire; at once our rifles flew to the present, and a volley clear and distinct rang on the desert air. The distance had evidently been miscalculated, for with only a few empty saddles on they came. Again our rifles blazed out, this time with deadly effect. Large gaps were seen in their ranks as horse and rider rolled headlong on the sand, and many a riderless charger careered madly from the field. For a few seconds they still came on, as if they had not realised the full effect of that leaden shower; but only for a few seconds, and then they turned and fled, even faster than they came, leaving behind them the ground strewn with their dead and wounded. We gave them a parting volley ere they disappeared over the hills, as a gentle reminder never to fly in the face of British infantry again.

Thinking that all danger was over, we marched back to camp, and busied ourselves catching the run-a-way fowls. We were, however, not destined to be left in peace, for in less than an hour we had to begin the most stubborn fight of the whole Egyptian campaign of 1882. I hope the reader will not confound the Egyptian war of 1882 with the Soudan campaign later on; as the battle I am now to record was not of the same type as such battles as El Teb, Abu Klea, etc. There the foe were wild and savage fanatics who gloried in death and hand-to-hand fighting, making those struggles of a shorter, but more fierce, desperate, and sanguinary character.

The railway was on our right, made up for a distance of half-a-mile, forming an embankment from 20 to 30 feet high. It ran parallel to, and some 200 yards from, the canal on our left. The intervening ground was rough and uneven. We formed deliberately up for the fray,

Battle of Kassassin.

having plenty of time, for the enemy, though in sight, were a good way off. As they came nearer and within rifle range, the smoke curled above their lines, followed by the "whish" of the bullets and the heavy roar of shells, announcing their challenge. Coolly we took up our position, under a galling fire, one half lining the railway embankment, while the other half extended to a thin line, each file two paces apart, at right angles and in the open plain, directly in front of the advancing host. It was a terrible contrast, and it seems a mystery how we ever managed to hold our own against such fearful odds. I think it was partly due to the Egyptians having a strong inclination to cowardice, and though quite willing to pepper us from a distance, were afraid of our bayonets. Here was one single line of British infantry, supported by only one 40-pounder mounted on a railway truck, opposed to 14,000 Egyptians armed with almost as good a weapon as our own, formed in three fighting lines, supported by massive columns of reserve, and 17 pieces of cannon. There was no thought of retreat, even had such a course been practicable, but the canal behind us barred the way. We must either do or die. Our company at the outset occupied the corner of the angle, and it was a lively nook. Immediately in front of us was our solitary cannon, now thundering forth in wild defiance. In return, a good deal of the artillery fire of the enemy was directed at it, with the view of disabling and putting it out of action. Bullets whistled close to our ears, their sharp "ping" only to be heard when they came within a few feet, as the continuous crash of exploding shells filled the air.

We waited till the front line of the opposing infantry was within 900 yards, and then opened fire with a vengeance. But the thinning process was going on; man after man, struck by the leaden hail, rolled down the embankment, clutching vainly at the sand in their descent. The comrade on my left, a bright young fellow, was shot in the shoulder, and as he leaned over to inform me of the fact, his rifle slipped from his hands, and he disappeared down the slope. Our captain also fell shot in the thigh. He was borne off to a place of safety by an Irish corporal, named Tim Dowling, and in the evening when Dowling and I visited the wounded, the captain presented him with his revolver as a token in lieu of the kindness he had received at his hands, at the same time telling us he would fight no more, as he had had enough of it. The half of my company were soon *hors de combat*, and General Graham, passing along and seeing that the position we were in was untenable, ordered us to proceed to the left flank, keeping the shelter of the railway embankment, and prolong the line nearer to the enemy. This was a welcome order, for our close proximity to our one cannon drew the fire upon us, and the enemy had evidently got the exact distance. Not only us, but the artillerymen also, had to shift and run their truck a few hundred yards along the line to throw them off their aim. Off we went, in sections, a few paces apart, and as we passed in rear of the fighting line, ever and anon down the declivity came the dead and wounded men.

Medical officers and staff were busy doing their best to ease the pain and dress the wounds of those brave fellows whose blood was ebbing away in their country's cause. I saw our own regimental doctor bending over a wounded man, when, with a cry, he threw up his hands, clutched frantically at the air, and fell on his back dead. He was shot through the head. Taking up our new post on the extreme left, we again poured in our fire. The

Battle of Kassassin.

position of the enemy compelled us to direct our aim to the left front, and each man's rifle crossed his comrade's face. The incessant hard ring so close to the ear was painful and deafening. We could scarcely hear the roaring shells; but every now and then a cloud of sand or pebbles would fly up in our faces, and we ducked our heads for the coming explosion, while all around the splutter of the bullets raised their little streams of sand. Just as one of those clouds rose in front, I received a stunning blow on the right side of the head, which sent the brain reeling, and the man rolling down the embankment. I lay for a few minutes in a semi-unconscious state, and then sat up and looked around on the ghastly sight at the bottom of the ravine which ran along below the railway side. My helmet lay beside me, the chain, which had been hooked up, cut in two, the thick puggaree round it to protect the head from the hot sun torn on one side to tatters, and part of the helmet itself away I knew not where. It was a near shave, and to the chain I believe I owed my life. It had turned the missile, and the thick folds of the puggaree had deadened the blow. As it was, I looked for the end, and strange thoughts flashed through my mind. All the stories I had read, of men receiving their death-wound without being aware until they suddenly lost consciousness and expired, came to my remembrance, and I prepared for the worst. But no; it did not come. Gaining courage, I put my hand gradually up, and it was with a feeling of indescribable relief that my fingers, instead of going into the hole I imagined, passed over a ponderous lump. I breathed more freely, and, sticking on my battered helmet, scrambled up to renew the fight, feeling little or none the worse of my expected transference to another world.

Battle of Kassassin.

Our shoulders were getting bruised with the continual recoil of the rifles, for we had each fired by this time from 200 to 300 rounds, and that too in a lying position. To relieve this, I saw several men rise in sheer desperation, caring little whether they were killed or not, and stand on the railway track in full view of the enemy, by this means easing the force of the recoil, which is not nearly so solid when standing as when lying on the ground.

I must, before going any further, record a few acts of bravery, or rather determination. The first was that of a young lieutenant, a mere stripling, named Cunningham, who, to use a Scotch phrase, "was game to the heels." He was running about distributing packets of ammunition to his company with hearty good-will, his face all the time wreathed in smiles, and though his voice was not heard, his manner indicated he was speaking cheering words, when crash went a bullet through his right arm. Nothing dismayed, the lad kept up the work with his left hand until a few minutes after he was shot in the leg and had to be borne from the field. Our sergeant-major, Carr—a strict disciplinarian, but still the idol of the regiment, for an ideal soldier always is—got one of his boots shattered, and his foot severely wounded by a fragment from a bursting shell; but he limped along, placing men here and there where he saw they were required. He must have been suffering great pain, though outwardly he showed no sign. Both Lieutenant Cunningham and Sergeant-Major Carr received medals for their bravery in this action. Our venerable and highly respected old colonel was passing up and down the lines, accompanied by General Graham, and though they cast an occasional wistful glance around, showed no trace of anxiety. If they saw any symptoms of weariness or despondency, they came forward and spoke a few encouraging words, telling us that reinforcements were on the way, and the day would soon be ours, and such like.

Officered by such brave men, of whom the above is only a sample, no thought of retreat could possibly enter our minds. It was clearly to be a case of death or victory, and we were ready for either, though, of course, we preferred the latter.

About 7 p.m. the enemy made a detour as if they meant to attack on the left flank, which, if successful, would have exposed us double-fold to their fire, for once they crossed the railway it would only be a matter of time to completely annihilate us by firing along the embankment. I must give honour where honour is due, and to a press representative belongs the honour of thwarting this flank attack. He was with our company on the extreme left, and for the time had given up his ordinary calling for that of a soldier. He had picked up a rifle, and, with his coat off, was blazing away. Some of us in joke told him to go on with his writing and never mind the fighting. His reply was, " Win first and write after; if you don't, there will be little need for writing." We all admired the conduct of this stalwart correspondent (he was a man fully six feet high), and if he reads this I have not the least doubt he will at once recognise himself. His eye was the first to see the white-coated Egyptians creeping over the railway line, and his stentorian voice was heard calling for men to follow as he sprang to his feet and ran along the embankment, followed by about a dozen of the men who were near and had heard his call. I was close to him, and, divining his intentions, also gave chase. We reached in safety a low mud wall which stretched across the ravine, and from this friendly shelter we mowed down the enemy with irresistible fury as they attempted to cross the line. Our stock of ammunition was almost run out, and before we got more some of us must run the gauntlet down this ravine for a distance of over 200 yards. My rifle about this time got jammed and refused to throw out the empty cartridge, and the gallant "reporter," whom we looked upon as our captain for the time being, said to me, " Corporal, your rifle is of no use ; take a man or two and off you go and get ammunition." We never once thought of disobeying him, and two men and I dashed off down the ravine. I confess to feeling rather uneasy at this running with my back to the foe. The bullets were whistling past, and being away from the noise of firing, their dull thud could be heard as they struck the hard sandy banks. We were glad when we reached and passed behind the fighting line of our comrades, for it was not then so awe-inspiring or dreary. There is no doubt that numbers help the courage greatly. Here, too, ammunition was getting scarce, and it was, I believe, 15 minutes before we got some 200 rounds gathered together and ready to set out on our way back. It was different altogether when going towards the foe ;. there is something inwardly exulting as you press on and the bullets crashing around you. Before we got half-way, both my companions were wounded, and I was undecided whether to go on or not, when I saw my former comrades retiring from their position, declaring that it was too dark to be of any use there. It seemed as if I bore a charmed life in that desperate ravine, for only two men and I out of the dozen that went up with the "reporter" came back safe. He received a bullet-wound in the side as he rose from behind the mud wall, and two men assisted him back. On the way he was again hit, while the soldier on each side of him got never a scratch. They conveyed

Battle of Kassassin. 75

him to a safer place, and he, though sorely wounded, informed the colonel after the battle was over about the brave conduct of the two men who brought him in, and they were congratulated at the head of the regiment next day on their bravery.

It was fairly dark now, and nothing of the enemy could be seen but the flashes of their rifles and cannons, and we fired in reply at random. Our ammunition being almost done, the firing waxed feeble, and unless we got relief our stubborn stand would be of no avail. As soon as our fire died away it would only be a matter of a few minutes for the superior numbers of the Egyptians to advance and crush us, for we were only a handful of worn-out men.

But two wise heads had been planning our deliverance, Lord Wolseley and General Graham. Though about ten miles apart, the bright flash of the heliograph had kept them in constant communication. About nine p.m. our bugles rang out, "cease fire!" Ignorant of the cause of the order, we nevertheless obeyed, though the enemy still blazed away as fast and furious as ever.

The pale moon was shedding her mellow light over the hard-fought field as we lay waiting for some fresh development, in what shape we knew nor cared not, for we had faith in our leaders. It was not long in coming. As if by magic, the noise of artillery and musketry ceased, and in its place came a tremendous British cheer. It was our cavalry charging through the Egyptian host. Thank God, we were saved! We could only see a black mass flying swiftly along, but the thunder of their horses' feet and their ringing cheers, mingling with the clash of sabres and the cries of terror and dismay from the enemy, told how terrible was the force of that brilliant charge. The battle was over, and the foe beaten and flying, pursued by our gallant horsemen, who captured the whole of their cannons, cutting the gunners down at their posts, so suddenly did they dash amongst them. Thoroughly wearied we marched back to camp, where we found a good supper ready, provisions having been sent on while the enemy were engaged with us. After it was partaken of, the companies' rolls were called, and it was with solemn looks we heard many a well known name shouted by the orderly-sergeants without the answering " here." There would have been a larger dead and wounded roll had we been a stronger party; the thinness of our lines and the cover of the railway saved a good deal of life. As it was, the killed and wounded amounted to about 100. I and some more went down to the side of the bridge where lay the wounded. The doctors were busy amongst them, and groans and cries of pain resounded on all sides. Some were in the throes of death; others bright and cheery, with legs or arms disabled. We did not stay long, simply bidding our best-known comrades good-bye, and then retraced our way to the camp.

The cavalry took up our out-post duty for the night, and, satisfied that we had fought a good fight and upheld the honour of our country, we lay down to rest and sleep.

CHAPTER X.

THE SECOND FIGHT AT KASSASSIN.

THE week following the battle recorded in the preceding chapter was a week of bustle and activity. Day after day reinforcements marched up to join us. Our long-lost tents, blankets, greatcoats, &c., also found their way to Kassassin, and now, when we were the proud possessors of several neat rows of white canvas, comfortable clothing to keep us warm in the cold mornings, and plenty of provisions, the thought of our former hardships were almost forgot. The Royal Engineers were utilising the railway line; two engines had been sent out from home, and, with the rolling stock captured from the enemy, were busy conveying to us the necessaries of life and war. Piles of food for man and horse were daily arriving, and between the unloading of trains, building up of those stores, throwing up ramparts to protect our artillery, &c., there was work for all hands.

In a few days our slender force had grown from two weak regiments and one gun to at least five regiments of infantry, two of cavalry, and some thirty pieces of cannon. Among the new-comers were two battalions of Belooches, from India — strong, powerful fellows they were, and seemingly full of fight. I had a rather unpleasant experience one evening while a number of us were on a visit to their lines. We had got hold of a few of them who could partly speak or understand English, and were fast making friends, when suddenly they made a rush on me, jabbering loudly all the time in their own language. Their weight bore me to earth, and, thinking I had given them some cause of offence for which they meant to punish me, I struggled desperately, and called lustily to my comrades for help. But no; they evidently knew what was meant, though I did not. After tugging and pulling at me for a little while, they released their hold, and I rose half choked and breathless. I must have looked very foolish, as roars of laughter broke out all around, which grew louder and heartier as the cause of the onslaught was made clear to me. It was this: I had been smoking a short time previously, and had put my pipe in my jacket pocket with the tobacco still on fire, and it had ignited my clothing. The Indians, seeing the smoke curling from my tunic, had each made a frantic endeavour to be the first to extinguish it. This, coupled with their unintelligible cries, had the effect of thoroughly scaring me. I had to listen to a repetition of this occurrence for many a day after—generally retold with a little colouring. There was also a regiment of Bengal Lancers in the camp, and they were a sight in themselves. Our cavalry seemed to glory in rusty stirrups and scabbards, while those of the Bengal Lancers glittered and sparkled in the bright light of the sun. They had a large retinue of followers who cleaned their accoutrements, and, generally speaking, followed and attended them wherever they went. Being seasoned to excessive heat, those troopers performed all the vidette duty on the hills; and as Tel-el-Kebir was only eight miles distant, they were continually getting into hot water with the Egyptian out-posts. Sometimes the whole regiment of them had to turn out and gallop to their sentries' assistance. On

The Second Fight at Kassassin.

these occasions they presented a noble sight as they swept past in two solid lines, the pendants on their long lances floating in the breeze, and the sun glancing from their burnished steel. They never drove in prisoners as our cavalry did; they always wounded them first, and then handed them over to their followers, who carried them into camp in their "doolies."

This method was followed because two of the dragoons that had fallen in the moonlight charge were brought in on the next day horribly mutilated, and the troopers swore revenge.

We were cherishing a hope that the enemy would see fit to attack us again, for we now considered that our numbers were sufficient to show them Kassassin in another light. Our wishes were not long in being realised. About 9 a.m. on the 9th September, 1882, I was on the top of a high pile of compressed oats and cut hay, counting the bales as they were carried up, when my attention was drawn by some of my comrades to the hills in the direction of Tel-el-Kebir. About $1\frac{1}{2}$ miles off, the Egyptians could be seen, again advancing in battle array; this time even in larger numbers than last. We were in for another tussle, and were all anxiety to be off to our own regiments to get into fighting order. There seemed to be no hurry, for not a bugle sounded until the advancing army was within a mile, and then the whole camp resounded with the notes of the "assemble." Before we got formed up the artillery on both sides were battering away at each other.

Our regiment was marched across the bridge, which was now fortified by earthworks, walls of biscuits in bags, and guarded by a battery of six 25-pounder guns. We extended in a skirmishing line and advanced along the opposite bank of the canal from the enemy, ready to prevent a threatened flank attack. After proceeding a short distance we halted and lay down, and such was our position that the whole field of battle was distinctly in view. Yet we had no risk, as not a bullet or a shell came near us. It was a grand sight: the artillery roared, the musketry rattled, while our heavy guns from their entrenched positions were vigorously replying. We saw the shells striking close to our gunners, and it was evident that the enemy had taken the exact range of the batteries on some previous occasion. To prevent this, our artillery " limbered up " and galloped out to the open plain, where their superiority soon manifested itself. After the first shot or two to gauge the distance, clouds of sand continually rose close to the Egyptian batteries, while they in their turn, now thoroughly out of their calculations, were firing wide of the mark. Our infantry were steadily advancing as though engaged on an ordinary field-day parade. As yet not a rifle had they discharged, though at one part of the field a regiment was resolutely climbing up the brow of a hill within 400 yards of the top where a portion of the enemy were. The cavalry were hovering on the right flank about two miles from us. Occasionally they made a wild charge in the direction of the now stationary lines of the enemy. This had the effect of gathering them together, which, when accomplished, the cavalry wheeled sharply to the side, and the artillery sent their murderous shrapnel amongst them. What a difference this field presented from the same field a few short days before. Then we were simply trying to hold our own, but now we had assumed the aggressive, and every moment saw the distance lessen between the opposing armies. In a quarter of an hour, if we remained where we were, and also the Egyptians, we would see the shock of the bayonet charge. Now, the white smoke curled thickly above the British force, and the din of musketry grew louder. At the same time came the order for us to recross the bridge and take up a position on the right of the whole line, at least a three miles' tramp. This crossing of the bridge was a ticklish task, for the enemy—undoubtedly with the intention of destroying it, and thus cutting off our water supply—were directing a heavy fire on its fortifications. We marched close in rear of our gunners, who were stripped to their shirts and trousers, loading and firing with might and main. Shells rent the air around, tearing their way through the walls of biscuit bags, sending the contents flying about our ears, and we quickened our pace to the "double." Across the bridge, through the camp and over the railway we ran, and then, breaking into quick time, we marched leisurely to our place on the right, having lost one man killed and three wounded in that brief run.

On our way to our allotted place we passed over for the first time the ground which had been occupied by the enemy at the recently fought battle. The Egyptians, although they had mustered courage to come back and take away the guns which had been captured at the cavalry charge, had not returned to bury their dead, and here they lay in hundreds, partly hidden behind the bushes of "benty grass," where they had sought a false shelter. It was a disgusting sight. The air stank with the loathsome odour of their partially-decayed bodies, and we were glad when we reached the outer edge and left them behind.

Long before we reached the main body of the army

the musketry had slackened and died away, for the Egyptians were beaten and in full retreat. The whole of our infantry halted and looked on at the flying foe. Not so the artillery. They were now in front, and firing away with right good will. Occasionally they would "limber up" and gallop nearer the enemy's batteries, when they in turn would retreat; but as soon as ours halted, and brought their guns to bear on them, they followed suit. This running warfare was carried on until the Egyptian artillery took shelter in the trenches of Tel-el-Kebir, the dim outline of which could be seen about four miles away.

A brilliant cavalry charge was all but executed before our eyes; at anyrate it was not the fault of our horsemen that it broke down. A large body of mounted Bedouins were observed about a mile to the right front bearing directly for about a fifth of their number of the 19th Hussars. We expected the Hussars to take protection behind us, and were waiting the order to "prepare for cavalry," when, to our astonishment, away dashed the small band of gallant horsemen to meet the swiftly advancing horde. Nearer and nearer to each other drew the opposing squadrons, and in a few minutes we expected to see the crash of battle as they met. But no; it was not to be. When some 400 yards intervened, a bright gleam of light flashed around the Hussars as their swords glanced from their scabbards and were carried aloft. Their horses seemed to catch the enthusiasm of the riders, for with outstretched heads, they quickened their already mad gallop. The Bedouins, apparently appalled by the compact ranks, surmounted by that halo of glittering steel, wheeled about and galloped furiously back, pursued by that bold handful of British cavalry.

The Second Fight at Kassassin. 83

We remained on the sandy hills during the most of that day. Eager consultations went on at different times between Lord Wolseley and staff, and it got rumoured amongst us that we were to attack Tel-el-Kebir there and then. Luckily it turned out to be only a rumour, for in the broad light of day, with the enemy keenly on the alert, Tel-el-Kebir would have been a hard nut to crack. Our colonel, with great forethought, had ordered the water carts to be filled with coffee instead of water, and under the broiling sun, tormented by countless thousands of flies, we partook of a coffee and biscuit dinner, sharing and exchanging coffee for water with our gallant companions the artillerymen. Before nightfall we marched back to Kassassin, having suffered but slightly in this fight, not more than 5 or 6 men being killed, and 50 to 60 wounded, including all the different branches of the service. Reinforcements were daily arriving, and among them came a number of army reserve men, straight from the green fields of England. They brought with them the latest home news, which was welcomed as only soldiers face to face with the enemy in a far-off foreign land can welcome it. On the afternoon of the 12th September, 1882, orders were given that, when darkness set in, all tents were to be struck and carried to the railway side, for we were to march that night—to where, we were not told, but we rightly guessed. When the black shades of night had closed around, quietly and quickly the camp was demolished, and, without sound of bugle, we took up our places, ready to commence the night march to Tel-el-Kebir.

CHAPTER XI.

BATTLE OF TEL-EL-KEBIR.

I DO not pretend, nor do I intend, to give the history or record the whole details of the weary march or the wild charge over the trenches of Tel-el-Kebir, as both have been written over and over again. It must also be borne in mind that a soldier in the ranks has but little opportunity of knowing the movements of other regiments at different parts of a battlefield, more especially in this case, where the operations were mostly hidden by darkness, and spread over a large extent of ground.

I simply follow the fortunes of my own corps or that of any other which came into touch with it, depicting the scenes according as they presented themselves to me.

Instead of the usual sharply-uttered command, "quick march!" by which we were wont to start, came the low and subdued tones of the various officers directing their companies to move forward. Crossing the railway, we commenced our march over the soft and powdery sand, which, fanned by a light breeze and scattered by many feet of horses and men, rose about us in heavy clouds. Between it and the darkness of the night we could scarcely see more than four yards around; it was a case of feeling our way. Ere a mile had been traversed we emerged on to harder ground, and the choking dust was left behind. Above was the clear blue sky, studded with innumerable stars, by some of whose twinkling light we were guided on our way. The columns had now sepa-

Battle of Tel-el-Kebir.   85

rated, and none of the other portions of the moving array were in sight. By and by a dark mass came in view on our right, and soon after the first halt was made. We stood for fully half-an-hour, while the staff officers in charge of the march rode slowly along to see whether every regiment and battery was in its proper position. We had deviated from the true course, as we had to bear off to the left about 100 yards before the onward march was resumed. The pace was slow—sometimes hardly moving, and never more than one and a half miles per hour. Every now and then we were brought to a standstill, until the same regulating process was gone through. I observed that we passed a number of upright stakes, about ten feet high, driven in the ground, and painted after the style of a barber's pole, which, I rightly presumed, were the guiding signs for the commanding officers. It was a weary, solemn night; the silence and darkness, combined with the nature of the task we were undertaking, gave us plenty of room for thought, and the thought that the coming morning might be our last kept uppermost in the mind. Those who had homes and loving hearts there, were whispering instructions to comrades to write and tell them the news of their fall; while names and addresses of those far-off friends were pencilled on scraps of paper, and freely exchanged. By midnight, strict injunctions were issued that not even a whisper would be allowed, nor a match struck upon any consideration.

As we moved slowly on, halts became more frequent, and, overcome by the weary dragging pace, sleep would steal over us, only to be immediately dispelled by a shake from some one near, recalling our senses back to the stern duty before us. A good deal of excitement was occasioned by a man who had been indulging in one of those short and troubled naps. He had apparently been dreaming of the rough field of battle, and must have fancied that the enemy were upon us, for he sprang to his feet with a wild cry, which caused the whole regiment to start up, and stand to arms. He was instantly seized and held firmly down, while some of his comrades placed their hands over his mouth until he came to his proper senses. After this we were debarred from sleeping ; officers and non-commissioned officers got strict injunctions to keep a watchful eye over their companies during those halts, to prevent a like occurrence, for we must be nearing Tel-el-Kebir, and the whole plans might be destroyed and rendered futile, besides the loss of thousands of lives, if the Egyptians had discovered us at that time.

On we went as quietly as it was possible for men to go. The others must have been doing the same, for not even the trampling of feet could be heard, and it seemed incredible that in front and around us 13,000 men and over 3000 horses were moving over that vast plain, but such was the case.

A grey tinge was slowly breaking in the clear sky overhead, and yet no signs of the foe. We had come to the conclusion that they had left their position and retired on the fortification at Zagizig, some miles further away, when, sharp and distinct, directly in front, there rang out on the still air three rifle shots. Two seconds scarcely elapsed till they were followed by three more, about half a mile to the right, and again a long way off, but from the same direction came the duller reports of other three. The Egyptians must have been in their trenches ready for the attack, and only waiting the signal, for scarcely had the sound of the ninth shot reached our ears, when, with

Battle of Tel-el-Kebir.

the rapidity of a thunderbolt, the whole place for miles in front was lighted up by one blaze of fire, while the roar of cannon and the din of musketry was terrific. Over our heads flew the bullets in a steady stream, with a sound as if sheets of iron were hurling through the air. The regiment, at the first blast of this fierce fire, shivered, staggered, and reeled from the force and unexpectedness of this terrible hail. Our gallant commander, Colonel Richardson, C.B., slipped from the saddle, his cheek shattered by a rifle bullet which struck him in the mouth and passed out below his right ear. (Though sorely wounded, he lived to rejoin us about a year after in time to lead us over the cataracts of the Nile in quest of the "Noble Gordon.") The sight of our brave colonel being assisted from the field roused our British blood, and we strained at the reins of discipline like blood-hounds on the leash in our wild desire to advance on the avenging track.

A minute or so elapsed before the next senior officer was aware of and realised the responsibility that had so suddenly devolved upon him, and for that brief period, as if to get protection from the leaden hurricane, we instinctively lay down and braced ourselves for the final charge, which, even without instructions, we knew was close at hand. At this juncture I found myself near to one of my best chums, an exceedingly jolly and hearty fellow, named Corporal Clark. Almost immediately he turned round to me and said, "He has done for me this time." I replied "who;" "Arabi," said Clark, with the utmost composure. At the same time he unslung his big clasp knife from his neck, and, handing it to me, asked me to cut away the trousers from the wound to ease the pain. He shifted his position slightly to come closer, and almost simultaneously a shell crashed through a bush of tall, white, grassy material, which he had unconsciously been reclining behind, sweeping most of it away with whirlwind force. This is one illustration of the many hairbreadth escapes which occur on every battlefield, for had Corporal Clark (or " Nobbie," as we generally styled him) not been wounded and moved from behind that bush at the exact moment he did, the next would have been his last. I took the knife from his hand, and gently commenced to cut the bloody trousers above the wound, which was in his thigh, when he, thinking I was handling him too gingerly, snatched it from me, and holding his trousers with one hand, with the other, he, by one quick, rough slash, laid the bleeding part bare. This hardly occupied a minute, and our new commander was already at the head of the regiment giving the order to extend to the left, which, for the benefit of the uninitiated, means to form a line of two ranks, and be ready to attack. Under the fearful canopy of lead that was still driving past, company after company doubled quickly and coolly to its place in the line with a steadiness that would have done credit to a review.

Luckily for us that we were not seen by the Eygptians, or a different tale might have had to be told. They were firing at too long a range—no doubt thinking we were further off than we really were; 6 or 8 feet above our heads it would have been almost impossible for man to live. I noticed that bullets were whistling across in front of us, w..ich made it impossible they could have come from the enemy, and in the darkness some far off portion of our troops must have been firing in the wrong direction. I am not aware where the order came from to fix bayonets and charge. I think it came by instinct. We heard the "clicking" of the fixing running along from the right, and we followed suit, marching forward all the time. We had

Battle of Tel-el-Kebir.   89

strict orders not to fire. The pace quickened to a run, and now we passed several dead or wounded Highlanders stretched on the bare sand.

Day was breaking. We could see the outline of the trenches some 200 yards ahead, girt with their sheets of living fire. Towards them the ground rose with a gradual slope, and a dim shadowy line of troops was rushing headlong within 80 yards of this hell of flame. The light was not yet sufficient for us to distinguish who they were, but we knew by the fallen men we passed that it was the noble Highland brigade dashing on to the charge, hence our injunctions not to fire. Faster we ran, and now outlined against the horizon close in front of us, in a wildly charging mass, were the first line of British soldiers — bayoneting, clubbing, and dealing death and destruction in a terrible manner among the Egyptian army. The next moment we leapt over the broad ditch into the pile of soft sand behind. This giving way under our feet, many were precipitated back into the trench ; but with the assistance of comrades they soon got out and followed on. Joining the already victorious Highlanders, and firing occasionally as we rushed on, we reached and scrambled over the second line of trenches, our red and bloody bayonets clearing the way, and in fifteen minutes from the time of the first shot we stood, flushed with victory, on the hills of Tel-el-Kebir.

It was now broad day-light, and the havoc we had wrought lay spread out before us. The dead and wounded lay in hundreds — some with frightful bayonet wounds ; others, having been shot at point-blank range, were rolling in agony, the clothes slowly burning on their bodies, and out of compassion these were immediately despatched. A number of tents were near by, and they

Battle of Tel-el-Kebir.

were cleared of the lurking and treacherous enemy, who, though beaten and half-dead, in several instances were seen to raise themselves on their elbows and take aim at the passing soldiers. Those who attempted this, sounded their own death-knell, for a sharp stab with the bayonet was their reward, and their life-blood ebbed quickly out on the sand. I witnessed one of those acts of treachery and unthankfulness on the part of a wounded Egyptian, which, had we been men of a fierce and bloodthirsty race, would have caused us to stamp the name of Tel-el-Kebir on the hearts of the sons of Egypt in such a manner that they would have looked back to it with even more bitter feelings than they now do.

A Highlander, on passing a wounded Egyptian, who was apparently rolling in the agony of death, paused, and bending over the prostrate man, raised his head, and applied a water bottle to his lips. The pain-racked soldier drank eagerly, and then lay back with a refreshed and satisfied look. The Highlander strode on, conscious that he had done a good and noble action, for he is always a brave man that readily extends his help and sympathy to a vanquished enemy, but he had not gone 10 paces, when I and some more who were looking on saw the Egyptian stretch out his hand and grasp his loaded rifle which lay near, then, poising himself on his elbow, take deliberate aim at his benefactor. A cry from us caused the Highlander to look back, just in time to hear the whiz of a bullet pass his ear. This was too much to bear, and the nearest soldier rushed forward and buried his bayonet in the treacherous foe. Such was one of the many instances of ungratefulness that occurred on the battlefield of Tel-el-Kebir.

It takes all sorts of men to make an army, or rather an

Battle of Tel-el-Kebir.

army is made up of all sorts of men ; for while some were looking on or aiding in the work of destruction, many were busy filling their pockets with valuables picked up about the tents. The ground was strewn with weapons of war—rifles, pistols, swords, etc. Some of those smaller weapons were moulded and finished in chaste and elegant design, while others, by their clumsiness, showed that they had been fashioned by workmen of the later ages, who knew not how to manipulate the material. Numbers of these were pounced upon and stowed away to be borne off as mementoes of this morning's stern work.

CHAPTER XII.

AFTER THE BATTLE.

HE attack had been carried out simultaneously along the whole length of the Egyptian fortifications (which were some seven miles in extent) with equal success and brilliancy, for on the wide plain below, scattered and flying, were thousands of the white-coated and vanquished foe. Our position was the best for obtaining a full view of the field, and one could not look in a thinking mood without being struck with the completeness of the plans for the attack.

The trenches stretched along the tops of low sandy hills in a sort of crescent form, while at intervals were substantial redoubts from where only a few short minutes ago the guns of the enemy, manned by the only gallant branch of the Egyptian army, viz., the artillerymen, had been thundering forth in all the fury of war; but, now silenced and in our possession, with their brave workers lying hashed and bleeding around them, they having fought to the last. The infantry had charged at different places on the outside of this crescent, thereby sending the beaten foe inwards. On the extreme right were drawn up in line about 40 pieces of cannon, placed so as to sweep the ground along the whole front. The cavalry were far away in the distance, detached in small squadrons, and galloping across the only line of retreat. On the left, about half a mile off, were the Naval Brigade with their gatling guns.

There seemed to be only one way for the Egyptians to get out of the trap, and that was by swimming the canal (which ran along the left of the whole operations), which numbers of them made for. But, though unseen from our position, the keen eye of Lord Wolseley had provided for this, by planting on the opposite bank the Indian Brigade and the Bengal Lancers. Completely hemmed in on every side, and torn almost to pieces by a heavy discharge from the iron throats of 50 cannons (even after they were in full retreat), they were effectually dispersed and disorganised. For perhaps ten minutes this merciless torrent of grape and canister kept ploughing its way through the retreating mass, and then came the order to " cease fire ! " It must have come as a god-send to these poor fellows who were wandering aimlessly about in the wide plain with the murderous shot mowing them down like wheat before the sickle.

Two or three companies of our regiment had marched to the left to assist the Naval Brigade in repelling the backward rushes of the enemy's cavalry in their frantic endeavours to escape, and sharp-ringing volleys from that quarter were still to be heard; otherwise all was silent.

Our artillery now limbered up their guns and came galloping across in front of the mixed up British regiments; for at least half a dozen different battalions had got jumbled up together during the charge at the place where we were. Over the rough uneven ground they tore —the drivers on horseback waving their whips and wildly hurrahing. Their horses needed not the lash, for the excitement of the battle had seized them also, and with the white breath flying from their extended nostrils they rushed madly on. The gunners clung to their seats with one hand, and waving the other joined in the cheer. It

After the Battle.

was too much for us to see those fine horses and brave men sweeping past so majestically without raising our voices in admiration and encouragement, and from thousands of British throats there rang a victorious cheer, such as the blood-stained hills of Tel-el-Kebir never heard before, and the natives never want to hear again.

The batteries were off to take up a position overlooking the railway, and thus prevent trains passing along the line in the direction of Cairo. Right well did they perform their task, for no sooner was their heavy boom heard, than a terrific explosion shook the very ground. Whether it was an engine smashed or a truck of ammunition exploded I know not, but a vast column of white smoke slowly rose towards the clear blue sky, and the line was blocked. Every now and again another such explosion broke on our ears from different parts of the field, but what caused them I am unable to say. The fighting being over where we now were, the buglers of the various regiments were called out and placed some distance apart, and as each one sounded his own regimental call and "fall in," the mass gradually separated, and in a short time stood in compact battalions ready to march down to the enormous Egyptian camp at the canal side. We drove the beaten foe before us, while the cavalry were quickly closing in, forcing them back until at last they were gathered together in one vast group, thousands strong.

The first thing to be done after we halted was to call the rolls, so that the list of killed and wounded might be flashed along the wires to our own land (where many a one was anxiously waiting); but for a time it had to be given up, as many of those who were marched to the left had not yet returned, and we knew not how they had fared. As it was, a good number of men of the different corps were sleeping the sleep that knows no wakening; and one might think that the death and mangling of comrades-in-arms so recently would have cast a gloom over even the victory. But no; soldiers get hardened to it, and the remark is passed "So-and-so is gone, poor fellow, I am sorry." The words were scarcely out of the mouth ere his fate seemed to have faded from the immediate memory. At anyrate, nobody could have said that sorrow had laid its heavy hand on our hearts had they seen us two hours after the battle. We were foraging through the Arab tents, gathering curiosities, looting provisions, of which there was an enormous quantity, picking out only the very best; for with plenty before us we were hard to please. Every now and then some of our missing comrades would come galloping into camp mounted on superb Arab chargers, which they had got without a master, or perhaps sent their masters across the "border," and then stole the ownerless steed. Whichever way they became possessed of them, it matters little; there they were in proud possession, and they seemed to know it, for their faces beamed with a satisfied smile as they trooped in, their rifles slung over their shoulders, while many of them were brandishing aloft the bow-shaped swords of the wild Bedouins.

The village of Tel-el-Kebir lay to the left of the canal, about a quarter of a mile off and on the opposite bank; but a bridge spanned the water, and again the poultry began to appear in camp. Worse still, an occasional goat strayed in amongst us on the shoulders of a soldier. Those animals being bulky, were quickly despatched and hidden in big tin boxes over roaring fires of wood, and I am safe to say by noon there were few hungry men in my company. If there were, it was their own fault. Lord Wolseley and staff had been busy during the forenoon with weightier matters, but he, or some one in authority, at last detected our little game, and a body of military police were sent to clear the village. When this was done, sentries were posted on the bridge, and the fun in that direction was over. Several times a rumour flew like wild-fire through the camp that Arabi himself was captured and brought in by the cavalry. This caused a general stampede to the spot, only to find we had been hoodwinked, as by this time he was speeding on his way to Cairo with the dragoons in hot pursuit.

In the early afternoon work commenced. Scores of trucks laden with ammunition (enough to destroy a kingdom) were standing on the line, and our regiment was told off to assist at unloading them, so that they might be utilised to convey troops to Cairo. Alongside the railway where they stood were large and deep sand or rather mud holes, capable of holding tons upon tons of shot and shell. From the trucks, we placed planks into these holes, and the boxes of ammunition were guided gently down. Familiarity, it is said, breeds contempt, and so it seemed in this case, as at first we were afraid to loose our hold on the boxes until they had reached the bottom, for fear of an explosion by rough usage; but, in less than two hours, we were placing them on the planks and sending them swishing down until they landed with a crash amongst those already there.

I met with a rather laughable occurrence during the evening, though at the time it was no laughing matter to me, and for long after I did not relish to hear it repeated, but time has effaced that now. It happened so: A soldier had been disobeying the order of a sergeant

After the Battle. 97

while working at the trucks, and I was ordered to march him to the guard-tent to be dealt with by the commanding officer. I got a file of men, and we were jogging over the sandy ground towards the camp, when a wounded and infuriated camel, maddened by pain. came across our track. With foaming and gaping mouth it rushed at us, and we scattered and ran for dear life, the prisoner one way, the escort another, and the camel after me in another. I had no arms to resist the attack ; there was nothing for it but run, and run I did with the ungainly beast in full chase. It was too swift for me, and several times I felt the hot breath at the back of my neck and its wild roar in my ear. I doubled again and again, and so gained a little way ; but it showed no signs of giving up the pursuit. The thought that I had escaped through the hail of many bullets only to be worried or trampled to death by a mad camel was unbearable, and I yelled for help. Those who were witnesses (and they were many) were filled with different feelings, for on nearing them I heard their hearty laughter, but an officer of some regiment (I know not which) grasped the true sense of the situation, and, rushing to the rescue, shot my pursuer. On marching back to the regiment, amid peals of laughter, I was greeted with numerous enquiries as to where my prisoner had gone, &c. It turned out to be a lucky chase for him, as he never heard of his disobedience again. He used to say that the hand of Providence would not allow a British soldier to be punished that day, and sent him deliverance in the shape of a mad camel. For two or three days we laboured among ammunition and wounded Egyptians, and then took train for Cairo. The war was over sooner than we anticipated, and Tel-el-Kebir was won with only the loss of about 400 men killed and wounded. The nation may thank Lord Wolseley for this, as to him it was indebted for the saving of thousands of brave lives. Had the attack been less skilfully planned or less skilfully carried out, Britain might have been mourning over a defeat on the 13th September, 1882, instead of a brilliant victory.

Part of the success was undoubtedly due to the cowardice of the Egyptians, and their want of proper outposts, for it was the openly-expressed opinion that, had our force been behind those splendid entrenchments, not an army in the wide world five times our number would have driven us out.

CHAPTER XIII.

CAIRO AFTER THE WAR: GRAND MARCH PAST; DEPARTURE OF THE HOLY CARPET.

THE journey to Cairo was slow and tedious. As yet the country was in an unsettled state, and treachery might be at work on the line; therefore it was necessary to proceed with caution.

The first town we arrived at was Zagizig, about 18 miles from Tel-el-Kebir. It was a fair sample of the other inland towns of Egypt (excepting Cairo), being, like them, a maze of narrow, crooked lanes and dirty mud hovels, with the round domes of a few mosques rising above. Thousands of dirty-looking natives were gathered about the corners and railway station, dressed in all conceivable sort of garments. Some were clad in long white or blue gowns and turbans, others had only a rag round their loins, and many of the younger generation devoid even of that. They stared at us with a savage expression, for, though we were there to protect them in a sense from themselves, and had succeeded, their countenances unmistakably showed their hatred. During our short stay here, we were pestered with them crowding round the trucks (not carriages, mind), offering for sale fowls, both roasted and boiled, eggs, melons, dates, &c. Those who had money invested in the dates and melons, but the fowls and eatables were ignored, we having no faith in Egyptians as cooks. The sight of their greasy fingers handling the food was quite sufficient to turn our appetites against it, unless we had been very hungry, which we were not.

Before night, we sighted the Pyramids standing grimly up against the clear blue sky, some 40 miles off, which may give the reader a slight idea of the levelness of the country, and the height and size of those wonders of the world, of which more anon. Shortly after it got dark the train stopped for the night, our officers deeming it imprudent to proceed, as under cover of the night the line might be tampered with.

By the first streak of day we went on, passing a number of towns by the way (all after the same pattern), and about mid-day we steamed slowly into the large and well equipped station of Cairo. Crowds of people were gathered, but had it not been for the prevalent tarboush (head-dress) and an occasional blue gown and turban, there was little difference from a railway station in our own land. Ladies and gentlemen of European birth and in European costume floated about the platforms with pleasant faces, for they were glad to see the British soldiers in their midst. They had passed through a trying time. Not being so luckily situated as their brethren in Alexandria, who had the broad Mediterranean beside them on whose bosom they could fly, those Europeans of Cairo, with their retreat cut off by the massing of the Egyptian army at Kafr-el-Dowar, had lived from day to day in danger of their lives, until our cavalry dashed into the town and captured the leader of the insurrection. Leaving the station, we made our way through the streets for about two miles; then crossing the river Nile by a substantial bridge some 300 yards long, we marched on to a rough sandy waste, named Gizeereh (directly opposite the centre of the city), and there encamped.

Cairo after the War.

We were favourably impressed with this the capital of Egypt. The streets through which we had passed were mostly in the European quarters, and several of them had a fine appearance, being composed of handsome houses, surrounded by lovely grounds and splashing fountains. Occasionally we got a glimpse of a street in the Arab quarter as we came along, and there all was ugliness and squalor. The bridge we crossed was also a masterpiece of work, and, taking all in all, we began to think that, even in this land of backward civilisation, houses and bridges could be built, and that too in an elegant and substantial manner.

We had rather a rough life in our new camp. Sandstorms were of frequent occurrence, and while cooking operations were going on, clouds of it whirled about the camp kettles, with the result that the soup was sometimes a curious mixture of vegetables, beef, and sand. If you wanted to take your dinner without feeling the rasping of portions of an Egyptian desert among your teeth, thereby sending a shivering sensation through the nerves, you had to allow your food to slide gently down, and beware of chewing.

I have often thought that, during the four years our regiment was in Egypt and the Soudan, bushels of this over-abundant sand had been transferred from the deserts to the stomachs of the men composing the Duke of Cornwall's Light Infantry.

As regiment after regiment arrived and pitched their tents beside us, Greeks, Italians, etc., followed and rigged up wooden huts and booths, wherein, by selling refreshments and all manner of other goods, they tried to, I was going to say, earn an honest penny, but I would be nearer the mark if I left out the word honest, for those fellows did not scruple to cheat if they got a chance. However, to do so they had to keep their wits about them, as it was no easy matter to cheat or swindle the British soldier, especially if he has travelled and roughed it a little through the world.

One enterprising Greek, who was the possessor of a wooden shanty wherein he sold, among other things, " laager beer," one day tried to cheat, and then, to make matters worse, raised the price of his beer. The following night his whole erection was rolled down to the bottom of the bank on which it stood, and the contents were never seen by him again; only a few empty barrels and boxes met his enraged eye the next day. He swore vengeance, and made off to interview the various commanding officers about his losses, but the only result was that no more beer-sellers were allowed to pursue their calling in our vicinity.

The daily arrival of regiments was causing the camp to spread over a large extent of ground. Acres upon acres were covered with neat rows of white tents, and soldiers in thousands strolled about the environs of Cairo.

About 4 p.m., on the 28th September, 1882, we thought the war had again commenced. The sound of a loud and terrific explosion shook the city, and it was followed by a perfect fusilade, seemingly of musketry, mingled with heavier reports as of bigger guns. Alarming rumours flew through the various regiments, and every man was looking to his arms and ammunition in full expectation that an outbreak on the part of the Egyptians had occurred somewhere in the town, and murder was going on. For a time we were at our wit's end: no orders came, and still the reports grew faster. Soon, in

Cairo after the War. 103

the direction of the railway station, the sky assumed a bright, reddish tint, and, as darkness set in, flashes of lurid flame cast their radiance around. It turned out to be an explosion of a truck in a train laden with ammunition, by what means was never (at least to my knowledge) ascertained. We put it down to incendiarism, because it happened at the very moment that the 60th Rifles entered the station on another train. The result of this explosion was that the whole train took fire, and the reports we had heard were the explosion of the shells and cartridges. The flames spread to the station building, which was almost burned to the ground; and, worse still, several soldiers were killed, and about 30 wounded by the flying missiles.

The day following this mishap was spent in cleaning and polishing our uniforms and accoutrements, for on the morrow, the 30th September, the whole army of occupation was to pass before the Khedive of Egypt in review order. The main object of this out-turn of the forces was to overawe and instil into the dull native mind the overpowering strength of the nation they had been opposing. Another object (a minor one) was no doubt to give the ruler of Egypt and his subordinates a sight of the army that beat and sent their countrymen flying from the trenches at Tel-el-Kebir in such a short time on that eventful morning.

About noon on the appointed day the different regiments mustered on their respective parade grounds, in readiness to proceed to a large open space in the centre of the city, known as Abdin Square. Anyone who is acquainted with the forming up of large processions will all the more readily grasp the magnitude of the task of massing some 20,000 troops in the various streets to emerge at a given time from one outlet, in order of precedence, and follow each other in bodies without a break between them. This was what had to be done in this case. Not a soldier (except the bandsmen) could be seen by those on the square until the massed bands gave the signal, and then to their stirring music the Household Cavalry in all their glory careered proudly past the grand-stand, on which sat the Khedive, surrounded by the elect of Egyptian society. We could hear the continuous roll of the drums for fully three-quarters of an hour, every now and then changing tune as different regiments went past (every regiment having a tune of its own for marching-past purposes). At last a mounted officer dashed round the corner, and signaled to our commander to advance. Away we went in sections of fours from the side street we occupied into the main outlet leading on to the square, our front section close on the heels of the rear of the battalion in front. Directly No. 1 Company emerged into the open space, the command came, " Front form company!" which means to form two lines, shoulder to shoulder. Never halting, they led on. Ere they had gone 30 yards, the bands changed their music to that of our own regimental march-past, familiarly known as "Tread on the tail of my coat, aha." Company after company went through the same formation, and followed on. The well-known strains of this lively tune, to which we had so often listened, sent a feeling of martial pride through our nerves, and, with smart step and heads erect, proud of the regiment to which we belonged, forward we marched. I was on the right of my company acting as guide, and so intently were my eyes fixed on the marking flags, that I only saw a dim sea of faces as the grand-stand was passed. Not a soldier turned so much as his eye to one side, for was not the highest ranks of the human race of Egypt, and also many of other lands, gazing on him? and right well did Tommy Atkins perform his part. That thrill of pride that held sway in our hearts made the step firm and elastic, and, like solid walls, line upon line of British infantry, with tanned and sunburnt visages, swept majestically on. When the leading company had got about 50 yards past the saluting-point, the sharp command rang out, " Fours right ; left wheel ; double !" The remaining companies followed suit, and, in less time than it takes to tell it, the regiment vanished into its allotted street. Back to the bridge we went, and stood about half-an hour until it came to our turn to cross ; then, taking our place in the steady stream of troops, we reached the camp. The march-past was over. Thousands of natives had witnessed our movements, for in every street they crowded, with looks of wonderment and awe clearly traceable on their faces, as those living waves of Britons moved through their quiet thoroughfares.

The next few days were spent in idleness, visiting comrades in other regiments, and fighting our battles over again. We were not as yet allowed to cross the bridge to make friends with the male Cairenes, or make love to the black-eyed European and native beauties, some pleasing samples of which we had seen on the way to the march-past.

On the 5th October, however, we were called upon to again invade Cairo with military pomp. This time the display we took part in rather grated on our British hearts, and, if I remember correctly, it created a deal of hostile criticism in the press at home. It was the occasion of the arrival of the Holy Carpet, a highly-embroidered rag, which, in accordance with Mahommedan religion, was conveyed to the shrine of the prophet at Mecca yearly on the departure of the pilgrims for that most sacred of all cities in the Mahommedan's eyes. The ceremony was conducted in a large open place near the gates of the citadel, where we, along with several other regiments, were drawn up in a hollow square. It was an animated scene ; the natives flocked about in thousands, and, amidst the clash of music, a highly-decorated camel hobbled in sight, carrying on its hump a heavy load of cloth and gold. This was the carpet. A long string of camels followed, mounted on which were half-naked Sheykhs, behaving like a lot of maniacs escaped from an asylum. The camel that came second was bestrode by a Sheykh, the maddest of them all. His hair was long and dishevelled, and he rocked from side to side so much that I expected him every minute to topple from the hump to the ground. With a flare of music and tom-toming on drums we, by word of command, presented arms. To all this eastern tomfoolery the British soldiers stood at the "present," but the disdainful curl on their lips told that it was gall to their innermost hearts. Round and round went the procession, and then the sacred "mat" was escorted solemnly to the station, the bands playing the "Dead March" as a parting tribute. Vast crowds followed, and amidst the jabberings and tom-tomings of the natives, the train steamed out of the station, and we marched back to the camp with a feeling of shame that ever we had been ordered to take part in such a ceremony. It seemed as if we who had fought the Egyptians so recently were now pandering for their favour.

CHAPTER XIV.

THE PYRAMIDS OF EGYPT.

FOR about a week things went on in a humdrum sort of way. Gradually the area covered with tents was getting smaller as regiment followed regiment away from here to other lands, and daily we expected the order to leave. Before doing so, there was a general desire to visit some of the notable places in and around Cairo. First among these came the Pyramids, situated about eight miles further up the river Nile. Our interim colonel, having made up his mind not to allow this opportunity to pass of giving his men a closer view of those massive and ancient structures, issued orders to that effect.

Accordingly, one clear morning, in the month of October, 1882, we struck and packed up sufficient tents to accomodate us for one night, as we were not to return till the following morning. Then we "fell-in," fully armed and accoutred, waiting the order to march to those enormous piles of stones, which had been looming grimly in our sight for some time back. We had partaken of a fairly good breakfast, and a day's rations was either in our haversacks or "in the man;" at least I heard some of my comrades declare it was easier carried by the latter plan.

The colonel appeared on the scene, and after a short speech, impressing on us the glorious sight in store, and how lucky we were to see for nothing what many people travel thousands of miles and pay large sums of money to visit, he gave the command "Quick march!" and we tramped merrily along the palm-studded banks of the Nile, through crowds of Arabs and Egyptians with their long strings of camels and donkeys moving townward, heavily laden with the produce of the earth for the morning markets at Cairo. Numerous were the salutations we received from these swarthy turbaned sons of the East as they plodded past; and although we did not understand much of their jabber, the ever-recurring "Harak Syida, Johnny" came from their lips, which was promptly answered by us with "Harak Syida, Mahomet," being equivalent to our "Good morning." They invariably styled us by the cognomen of Johnny, and we retorted with Mahomet.

Following the banks of the Nile for about two miles, and then making a detour to the right, we entered on the direct route to the Pyramids. Flat and straight as an arrow lay the road in front, for fully six miles, made up some twelve feet higher than the land on either side, which at this season was partly inundated by the recent overflow of the Nile. At the opposite end, and looking only three miles off (so clear was the air and deceiving the distance) stood on the rising ground, on the borders of the sandy desert, the largest of all the Pyramids known as "Cheops."

Marching along, we were exceedingly annoyed at the vast numbers of young frogs jumping from one side to the other; they literally covered the ground, and it was difficult to set down our feet without treading on them. One man might have picked his way and left them uninjured, but 600 never. They lay behind in our track, crushed and battered in hundreds, and opinions were freely passed as to their presence there in such unlimited numbers. One fellow, a bit of a wag, hailing from County Devon, who had evidently in his boyish days often rehearsed the history of the plagues in Egypt, was explaining to his nearest comrades his theory as to how those plagues were brought and taken away again. I overheard him conclude his peroration in the following terms, accompanied by forcible illustration of " Aaron stretching forth his right arm over the land at Moses' bidding, and commanding them to come." " See here," said the wag, " Aaron stretched forth his arm to the full extent when he ordered these frogs to come, but, when sending them away again, his heart was not in it, and he only stretched half-way, and so left plenty for the future." That was his definition of the matter, not mine; I only record what I overheard ; but it remains a glaring fact to this day that several of the plagues which then reigned hold their sway to a great extent in the land of Egypt, notably amongst them being those of flies, frogs, and lice.

We passed several sand-banks rising from the water on both sides, and standing on them, motionless as statues, were the long-beaked and weary-like birds, the pelicans of the wilderness, the restraints of discipline only saving them from instant death, as more than one I heard express a wish to discharge the contents of a Martini-Henri at them (for which each man carried 100 rounds). Further away were a few collections of mud-huts comprising small villages, slightly beautified by the graceful palms clustering in their vicinity. The natives were busily engaged, some pulling boats from village to village, and to the road on which we were. Others had divested themselves of their scanty clothing, and, sometimes wading, sometimes swimming, were pursuing their ordinary vocations, which seemed to be, at this time of the year, carrying fruit, vegetables, fowls, &c., to the markets at Cairo. After about three miles had been traversed a good deal of grumbling could be heard in the ranks, for it is an inherent quality of a Britisher; grumble he must, whether circumstances justify it or not. First the march was too long, then we were too heavily laden, our day's ration was being eaten up, and still three miles ahead lay the Pyramids A day's exploring and climbing was before us, and no prospect of replenishing the store for the inner man till we arrived at our proper camping-ground the following morning. A short rest seemed to sooth the grumblers' feelings, for the march was resumed in better spirits. As we drew nearer and nearer to the Pyramids, the stones of which they were composed looked larger and larger, till what we had viewed with indifference from the camp now began to be regarded with admiration and awe, so vast were the dimensions of those structures. Halting at the foot of the sandy hill, near the water's edge, we pitched our camp, picketed our mules, and, leaving a strong guard in charge, the remainder of us wended our way in the direction of the mighty "Cheops." Venerable-looking residenters met us, who clearly claimed the Pyramids as their own exclusive property. They offered their services as guides at high figures, making us understand that we had no right to proceed further except with their permission, and under their guidance. They were all supplied with various articles, such as old coins, rings, &c., rusty and dilapidated, which they proudly held up to us for inspection and sale with the cry of "Very much antique, Johnny," at the same time informing us, in their broken English, that those relics had been dug from

The Pyramids of Egypt.

historical caves and tombs near by, where they had lain for thousands of years. One fellow walked up to me, and with the utmost composure held up what had once been a ring, but now simply a mass of rust, and said, "Pharaoh's ring, Johnny, takee from tomb, worth much English money, plenty bucksheesh." Needless to say, the history they told us fell on barren soil, for it is well known that these unscrupulous rascals collect their wares wherever they can lay hands on them, and even manufacture them for the occasion. Still, a ready sale is often got for these trinkets, as many people, when visiting this wonderful place, have their minds brought into a very pliable state, and between the solemnity of the scenery and the venerable guides in flowing robes and white turbans, with their eager pleadings, buy extensively of those so-called antiquities. Many of them are also holders of certificates as to their honesty and truthfulness, written and endorsed by the leading nobility of our own and other lands, in whose service they had probably been only a few hours at most. After my experience I imagine these credentials had been presented more with a view of getting rid of them, and their continual cry of bucksheesh than as to their character. However, this was to be a red-letter day for them. Tommy Atkins was in force, and ignoring assistance or guidance, determined to explore for himself.

For a short time it appeared as if the Battle of the Pyramids was to be fought over again. Those swarthy sons of the desert clustered round the end of the beaten track that led up the Pyramid as if to prevent the oncoming wave of red-coats. In a few seconds the opposing forces met in fierce strife, and Arab and Briton rolled on the sand in no very loving grasp. Numbers for once were in our favour, and the Arabs, seeing that resistance was useless, abandoned their position and beat a sullen retreat; and soon the vast sides of " Cheops " were thickly dotted with British soldiers climbing and struggling towards its summit from all directions. Here I may say that there are a number of Pyramids—some close at hand and more about four miles to the south east, but I confine myself to the largest and places of interest in its vicinity, merely remarking that, with the description of it, you have them all comprised, but on a larger degree than the others.

I seated myself on a rocky mound near its base, but at such a distance as to secure as full a view as possible, and I venture to say that neither pen nor pencil can convey to the mind of the reader the immensity of this phenomenon. It was built of massive blocks of soft grey stone, each measuring about five feet high by ten feet long, rising tier upon tier from a foundation covering 11 acres of ground to the height of 480 feet. The thinking visitor can do nothing for a time, but gaze and meditate, and his or her thoughts will go back to the whole history of this ancient land as given in the first books of the Bible. Aided by those immense works, the mind can more readily and clearly grasp the realistic character of what is therein recorded.

I left over the climbing till the cooler hours of the evening, the sun being now high in the heavens, and almost scorching us with its pitiless rays. Procuring the services of a guide, two comrades and I set off to see and gain information on the interesting objects in the immediate locality.

Through piles of granite and other stones we tramped, here and there built in the form of a wall, but abruptly broken off, as though for want of a plan. Those

The Pyramids of Egypt.

walls were a curiosity in themselves, for they were fashioned of enormous stones laid above each other with a remarkable degree of neatness, their ponderous weight having kept them in places for ages, without the aid of mortar. So close were the joinings that it was a marvel how it could have been done in those primitive days. I question if the builders of the present time, with all their modern skill and appliances, could do likewise. Passing on, we came to a sandy square about 15 yards wide, and encompassed by a ditch some six feet broad and 40 feet deep, all built of huge blocks of granite. Peering into each side in succession, we saw a number of recesses or shelves about half way down, made by large stones being hewn out in the centre after the manner of a watering trough, which our guide informed us were the tombs where some of the mummies now in the museum at Cairo had been taken from.

Leaving this, we arrived at the Sphinx, which is situated about 300 yards to the south-east, and on considerably lower ground than "Cheops." It consists of a block of grey stone of almost inconceivable size, cut in the form of a beast, its back rising above the sand which covers the lower part of the figure. A head carved in human likeness, but rendered demoniacal by its enormity, towers above from 20 to 30 feet. We stood looking up into the remorselessly haggard and time-eaten face, with lumps of stone chipped from every projecting part, evidently by visitors in their endeavours to carry away relics of their visit. Even now, as we looked, a few redcoats, with no veneration for Egypt's motto, were hurling at the broad countenance pieces of hard granite, knocking off chips, which their comrades were eagerly picking up to take with them as mementoes of their holiday. This is a wonderful monument, and one cannot look into the scarred and torn visage, with the sullen expression peculiarly its own, without experiencing a feeling something akin to awe; it is so monstrous, human-like, and yet un-human in its appearance, as it stands and has stood from time immemorial—a conspicuous monument of the sculptor's skill of ages long since passed away.

We next found ourselves at what is known as the "Temple of the Sphinx." Lighting a candle each, which our guide supplied, we entered and passed through a compactly-built passage, roofed overhead, which emerged into a lofty chamber of ordinary dimensions. The floor was of sand, but the walls were magnificent, composed entirely of alabaster and granite stones (dressed to a high degree of smoothness, but unpolished) laid above each other in alternate rows. Had it not been the difference in colour, the joinings would have been almost imperceptible, for I tried to insert the blade of my pocket-knife between them, and failed. This was the most beautiful place in the whole neighbourhood. The pure white of the alabaster contrasted and showed itself in brilliant relief as it lay in regular rotation with the more familiar granite. Numerous names of previous visitors were here written on the walls, and by the feeble light of three candles we added ours to the already long list, and then retraced our steps to the open air.

From there we made our way back to explore the interior of "Cheops." Coming round to the side facing Cairo, we climbed up the rough massive stones forming the lower part for about 30 yards until we reached the entrance tunnel. In went our guide, and we followed, for a short distance experiencing no difficulty, as the floor was level; but we had not proceeded far when it began to decline sharply downwards, making it impossible for upright walking, owing both to the declivity and the absence of anything to hold by The bottom stones were also very smooth, evidently worn with the friction of many feet passing up and down on the same errand as we were now bent. It was an exceedingly awkward place for safe locomotion, and had it been much wider there would have been only one way of getting along, and that by sitting down and sliding. But the width was such that we got our feet planted against the sides, and, with our hands placed on the stone floor behind our backs as a support, we crawled for a long way, headed by the guide and the solitary light of the candle which he carried—we having enough to do to manage ourselves. At the end of this declivity there was a drop of five feet, which was safely overcome. Lighting our candles, we picked our way through a tortuous pathway, at some places low and narrow, at others high and broad. Large stones lay directly in the way here and there, considerably retarding our onward progress, and a good deal of scrambling had to be done before we stood in what the guide said was the very centre of the Pyramid. It consisted of a large and lofty space arched overhead with ponderous stones firmly built, as they needs must be, seeing so tremendous a weight lay above them. Lying round the foundations were a few stones hewn out in the centre like those described near the Sphinx, which our guide, ever ready with information (though on account of his imperfect knowledge of our language much of it was scarcely comprehensible), made us understand were the tombs wherein reposed the mummies of the Pharaohs and other great men of the land, until they were discovered and taken away to other places. There was no regularity here; stones were strewn about on the sandy floor; and all bore an air of disorder. Here also were names of visitors carved and chalked on the stones, and ours found a place amongst them. This was a gruesome spot; the stillness was oppressive, and our voices rang on the walls with a weird unearthly sound, the feeble flickering of the candles barely breaking the intense darkness. Very few of our comrades came in here, for it was unsafe without the services of a guide; and if our one had run off, and left us, it would have been a difficult problem to find the way out. We made our stay short, and in a brief space were again breathing a purer air outside. We paid off our guide with a shilling each, and in addition gave him a pencil-written certificate bearing testimony as to the satisfactory manner in which he had performed his duties. He was quite pleased, and left us profusely muttering his thanks in such terms as, "English very good gentlemen, give Arab plenty bucksheesh; me likee English, &c."

Tired and weary, we made for the camp, entering *en route* a few small caves; but with the exception of curiosities in the shape of Egyptian hieroglyphics carved on the walls, there was nothing to detain us, and we were soon under the welcome shade of the canvas. Seeking out our haversacks, wherein were our provisions (not being amongst those who thought the ration easier carried "in the man") we partook of a hearty repast of American roast beef and hard biscuits, washed down by a plentiful supply of water from the neighbouring pools, and lay down to rest till the cool of the evening, when we meant to climb to the top of the rugged "Cheops." A few hours sufficed, and we rose refreshed and ready for our self-imposed task. Arriving at the Pyramid, we sat down and took off our heavy boots, thinking we would be

The Pyramids of Egypt.

lighter and more sure-footed without them ; but we sorely repented that before we came down again. Ledge after ledge we mounted, at first with considerable difficulty, as we had no guides to lend a helping hand, and the large size of the stones made each ledge about five feet above the other. But as we got higher up, the stones gradually got smaller, and therefore easier to surmount. For a time we toiled on, fully intending to reach the top before we halted ; but no ; we squatted about half way and had a short breathing space. On again, and this time we never wavered until we lay panting and breathless on its summit. But we had our reward. A most extensive and magnificent view of the richly-cultured delta of Egypt lay beneath us, dotted with its palm trees, cotton and sugar fields, intersected with canals, and tracts of water left from the overflow of the Nile. About eight miles off, and far below, lay the city of Cairo, its beautiful suburbs of noble mansions, pleasure-grounds, and palaces forming a picturesque panorama ; while distinctly outlined against the clear blue sky rose from the wide-spreading mass of buildings the tall minarets and domes of the mosques where the Mahommedans worship their God. On the edge of the desert overlooking the city was its stronghold, "The Citadel" (then occupied by British troops), its ramparts and lines of defence being clearly discernible from our point of vantage. The expansive track of the mighty Nile was visible for many miles, its waters sparkling and glistening in the silvery light of the now setting sun. On its bosom, ploughing their slow and steady way, were numbers of Egyptian Dahabeeyehs, their tall masts and rakish spars, loaded with broad sheets of canvas, some near, and some far away looking like models in the distance. Breaking the monotony of their sluggish glide were several steamboats passing more rapidly along, leaving behind them a trail of ruffled water and black smoke, as if to demonstrate that the impetuous forces of civilisation and modern improvement were dispelling the quietude, and sending energy and motion into this ancient land, where old customs are clung to with great tenacity. To the south or behind stretched the rough sandy deserts, almost bordering the banks of the river; but, as the Nile flowed nearer and nearer to its destination, they gradually receded, till, where the eye lost sight of them, they were miles apart, enclosing between them and forming, as it were, a framework to this beautiful picture of the fertile valley of the Nile. Few places can command such a range of vision as is obtained from this place. The country being level, there is nothing to impede the sight; the eye simply penetrates to the utmost extent of its power, and then loses itself in space.

A better estimate of the extent of our view can be arrived at if one bears in mind the fact, that when coming from Alexandria to Cairo, the top of this Pyramid can be seen when it is fully 50 miles away. A flag-staff was reared in the centre, and lying round it were a few stones, left as if the builders had ceased work before their material was all built, and had never resumed operations again. One of the party climbed to the very top of this pole in spite of our entreaties. If it had given way under his weight, he would have been hurled down the sides, and launched into eternity in an instant, for the Pyramid had gradually narrowed to the modest dimension of about six yards square.

Time was getting precious: the sun was fast sinking in the west, and in this land darkness comes on apace, so when our comrade slid down the flag-staff in safety, we

The Pyramids of Egypt.

commenced our downward way. This was a giddy and dangerous task. Coming up, the height was not so apparent, our eyes being directed upward, but now they were of necessity directed downward, and it was with slow and cautious steps that we treaded our path. Our feet, too, were getting sore from so much climbing without our boots, and glad were we when we reached mother earth again. Soon we were safely under canvas, and opinions were freely passed as to how those structures had been built, the one finding most favour being that the men of those days had been all "Samsons." Most of us had pieces of stones and other relics to take home, as mementoes of our visit, but few of them ever reached the hands they were intended for, as we knew not the fate in store; for out of 600 who climed the Pyramids on that well-remembered day, one half left their bones in Egypt and the Soudan. Sleep, sweet sleep, enveloped us in its folds, and when the bugles rang out the "Reveille" in the early morning, all was bustle and stir, packing the camp-equipment, and getting ready for our return journey. We reached the camp proper about 9 a.m., and the regimental cooks had a hearty breakfast prepared, which was as heartily partaken of, and our holiday in Egypt was over.

CHAPTER XV.

RECOLLECTIONS OF ALEXANDRIA.

ALMOST before we got breathing-time after the excursion to the Pyramids, we were despatched to Alexandria to take up our quarters there, as one of the five regiments left to represent our country in the land. I need not dwell on the route at any length, as it was weary in the extreme. I remember the night we spent in the railway trucks was bitterly cold, and though we were closely packed, our teeth chattered as the keen air pierced our light and scanty clothing. On stopping at the different stations on the line, the natives, evidently having found out that we belonged to a droughty nation, hung about the train trying to dispose of their abominable con-ē-ak. Of course we had strict instructions not to buy, but for all that many a shilling was handed down for bottles of the fiery liquid, with which we sought to raise the heat. When within some 20 miles of Alexandria, the train came to a stand-still, for some reason or other, and there remained till dawn. Then proceeding, we steamed slowly through the very centre of the trenches at Kafr-el-Dowar, and it only wanted a cursory glance to see that even the fortifications at Tel-el-Kebir were but mounds compared with these, to all appearance, impregnable defences. Soon after we arrived at Alexandria, and marched to Ras-el-tin Palace, where the regiment was to be temporarily quartered until barracks were fitted up for us at Ramleh.

Recollections of Alexandria.

For the following nine months I was completely severed from the regiment, being detailed to take charge of six men, and proceed to the head-quarter office, which was in an unoccupied house close to the station, where we loaded our baggage when on our way to Ismailia. General Harman (now Adjutant-General at the War Office), was then in command of the army of occupation, and as orderly, clerk, usher, &c., I attended on him until he left for home, while the men acted as messengers, and kept things in clean and ship-shape order about the offices.

The morning after our arrival I made the acquaintance of Colonel Clery, a most able officer, then chief of the staff (now also in a high position at the War Office.) The first order I got from that gentleman will always remain fresh in my memory, and I will give it to the reader in almost the very words that he gave it to me. There is a lesson in it which may show how some men get over difficulties when others would sink under them.

The house we occupied was in a state of disorder, owing to the hurried flight of the owner, and the ravages afterwards, and it was decided to have it thoroughly cleaned before we took formal possession. Therefore Colonel Clery told me to get a tent from my regiment (by his order) and pitch it at the end of the house for our use, until the cleaning operations were over. The tent was procured, and I. accompanied by my men, commenced to rig it up ; but we had not calculated on the formation of the soil, which was hard and stony, for after we had it reared, the wooden pegs wou'd not pierce the rocky ground, and a number of them broke under our hammering. We held a short consultation, with the result that I went back to the colonel and told him the ground was too hard to get the pegs driven in. The only reply I got was, " bosh ! go and pitch the tent ; I never send men to do what is impossible." Back I went with the news to my squad, that up the tent must go some how or other, and a man was sent to the station to borrow an iron hammer and puncheon to drive holes in the hard stony earth. After a deal of labour we completed our task, and about two hours later I met the colonel, who asked how I had got on : " Is the tent up?" " Yes, sir," I replied, and, as if to qualify my words, added, " but I had to borrow a hammer and puncheon at the station to make holes." " Well, hang it, did you think I was to go and borrow them for you." I never got an order from him after and went back to tell him that it could not be executed.

Our duties here were very light, and we had p'enty of time to roam about the streets. A vast change had come over the town ; it was now swarming with inhabitants from mostly all nations under the sun. A stroll through the Arab thoroughfares showed that already the war had been forgotten. The natives sat against the walls in their own cross-legged curious way, smoking their long pipes, while in front of the dark dens wherein spirits and coffee (the latter as thick as syrup) were sold, tables were placed in the streets, and seated on chairs, bending over a game of dominoes, were the white turbaned heads of those eastern gamesters, sipping their coffee, amid the rattle of the dice. Very seldom did we wander through those parts; the fierce looks bestowed on us, as we picked our way through the tables, were quite sufficient to keep us at a distance.

We found more congenial enjoyment in the European quarters. There the merchants and publicans were busy getting their battered premises in order, while temporary wooden huts to carry on their business were erected. The grand square was one mass of those huts, some large, some small; but all tastefully arranged inside. A "Royal Oak" bar sprang into existence in the centre of the square, the name designed undoubtedly to catch the British soldiers, and so it did, for in the evening it was generally packed. On a large stage at one end, a string, flute, and brass band combined, composed entirely of young and handsome girls, discoursed sweet music every night. When a tune or two was played, those lovely damsels would occupy their breathing space by sitting at the tables along with the gay soldier, helping him to quaff the foaming ale.

It was no uncommon sight to see a British soldier carrying on a lively flirtation with the big drummer.

There was another place of the same kind, but on a more elaborate scale, known as the "Cafe Paradiso." It was patronised to a large extent by civilians, especially on Sunday nights. On that night very few soldiers went there; it did not seem right to do so; one or two in passing might call in for curiosity. I was once there on Sunday night, and was greatly surprised to see men walk in with their wives and children, take their seats at the tables, order their refreshments, and settle down to hear a few tunes. The natives hardly ever darkened the doors of those places, except the higher class who had fallen into the European custom of clothing, and then it was no easy matter to distinguish the difference between them. The above were about the only places of amusement we had to go to, and rightly or wrongly, they did a roaring trade.

Now for the open air; donkey-riding was the rage. At every street corner stood donkeys, saddled and bridled, with their lanky-legged keeper close by, invariably a boy. One piastre (2½d.) was the recognised fare for about a mile, and, being a novelty, we seldom walked, except very short distances, so long as the money lasted. It was a laughable sight to see those lads standing with their patient animals about the barrack gates, and whenever a soldier appeared, there was a mad rush of boys and donkeys towards him. Each boy shouted out the qualities of his quadruped in such language as, " Me very good donkee, Johnny; one piastree ; dis donkee speak English, Johnny ; black diamond ; me donkee flying Dutchman, Johnny, take 'im, very good," and so on. If you stopped for only a couple of seconds to choose for yourself the clamour around you grew worse, and you were glad to jump on to the nearest and handiest one, and scuttle out amongst them. Such was off-duty life at Alexandria.

In the day time a walk through the streets showed that the work of rebuilding was going smartly on. Squads of men were busy on all sides clearing away the fallen *debris*; patching up some houses, building others from the very foundation, and gradually renewing the city.

One notable feature connected with this work was the employment of women as "labourers." They slacked the lime, carried stones up the ladders, and, generally speaking, kept the builders going. It was with astonishment that we beheld the sight of those Egyptian ladies (in their long bluish gowns, with a few inches of scarlet trousers peeping out below at their ankles, which were often adorned by a few copper-coloured rings) climbing up the ladders with their loads. Those women had a hard life. A grey-headed, sour-visaged native would perhaps have three or four wives engaged at this work. Seated on a donkey, with a long stick in his hand, he would drive them before him to their work, and, when night came, drive them home again, and on pay-day drew their pay for them also. The more wives, the richer the man. All reprimands for bad or too little work seemed to be applied with the lash as well as the tongue. The master or foreman of the different branches of labour could be often seen going up to one of the workmen, and, in the midst of a perfect torrent of words, bring a stick or whip across his shoulders with a terrific whack, and, with a scowling but thoroughly cowed expression, the poor fellow set to work in earnest, bestowing occasionally a sidelong glance at his beater to see if he was to repeat the dose.

Now for prayers; the Egyptians were truly religious, in their own way. At almost any hour of the day they could be seen on the house-tops, or in the streets, spreading out a cloth (if they could afford one). Then taking to their knees, they would go through a number of motions with regularity, commencing by placing their hands only on the ground, and bending the head; then the next motion: the forehead would come down until it also rested on the ground. This practice would be repeated slowly for about five minutes—all the time with their eyes shut, while they kept muttering away at texts from the "Koran." Now, although we do not recognise theirs as the true religion, there is one thing in connection with it that cannot be got over, and that is their firm, fearless, and open adhesion to their worship. The devotion shown by those deluded men is in striking contrast to, and far exceeds, the worship of the true God in our own Christian land.

There is a looseness and *sang froid* about the streets which is refreshing. For instance, you see a gentleman coming along in the morning; he is in want of a shave; towards him comes a small Arab youth from 13 to 15 years of age, carrying a large flat-shaped wooden basin, wherein lies an oval looking-glass with handle, a lather pot and brush, razor, and all the necessaries of the barber trade. A camp-stool is slung over his shoulders; he meets his customer, down goes the stool, and the customer takes his seat; a towel is spread round his shoulders, and in a twinkling his face is a mass of lather. Then with what nimble fingers the boy plies the razor. An English or Scotch barber would blush for his trade if he saw those Arab lads shaving. The keen blade flashes about the face with lightning rapidity; the operation is over, the money paid, and the gentleman rises and walks off, being only detained for about two minutes. All this takes place in the street, with people passing and repassing, but no notice is taken.

We will now have a passing glance at the roguish side of the inhabitants. Alexandria bears the palm (as well as the palm tree) of every city that it has been my lot to visit for swindling.

Bad and counterfeit coin is as plentiful as the genuine article Of course everybody has to learn by experience how to detect the spurious pieces, and the population being composed largely of the migratory class, as many people pass through every day as would afford a living to those inc'ined to cheat.

Men sit in the streets behind a small table covered with a glass lid. Underneath and above this glass lay piles of gold and silver, good and bad, mixed. These are the money-changers. You go to them for the first time to change say a pound (you can get it in the silver money of almost any country). Picking up what is counted out to you, you leave. But perhaps, soon after, on going into a shop to make a purchase, judge of your surprise when coin after coin is rung on a stone (fixed on the counter for the purpose), and handed back to you as worthless. The next time you go for change you take particular note of what you receive, by ringing every piece to ascertain whether you have the genuine article or not. There is no law forbidding this practice; therefore every man has to look out for himself. Many an unscruplous rascal makes a good livelihood by this traffic.

Not only is there a trade in bad coin, but many other means are adopted for fraudulently obtaining money. One forenoon, shortly after I joined the head-quarter staff, I was made the victim of a swindle, which I will relate as one instance of the extent to which cheating is carried on in Alexandria.

I was sent by Colonel Clery to the Custom-house, to get a parcel for him, which was lying there. He gave me two shillings to pay the dues, and also warned me to be on my guard, as in the vicinity of the Custom-house there was always a collection of rogues trying to extract money from the unwary callers. He was right, for as I arrived at the street or quay, where it was situated, and made my way towards the building, I was asked by a smart well dressed individual speaking good English if I was going to take out any parcels. I replied in the affirmative, whereupon he conducted me to a number of men who sat in the street with a writing desk before them. They had a quantity of papers with some printing on the top in French.

One of these was handed to me after the clerk had inscribed a few Arabic dots and curves on it. For this I was charged 6d. I demurred paying it, but my self-appointed guide told me he was in the employment of the Customs, and without paying for three of those papers I could not possibly get the parcel. He put the matter so honest-like and plainly before me that, after some hesitation, I handed over three sixpences to different parties, and in return got three of these papers. I was making my way to the door, thinking I was all right now, when my interpreter also demanded a 6d. for his services. I declined, and he at once called on a pompous gent'eman who was standing in the door-way (one of his own clan, but I did not know then.) He in his turn pretended to be one of the leading men of the Custom-house, and so impressed me that I parted with my fourth sixpence, and then went inside.

I found myself in a long passage, on both sides of which sat, in different compartments, about 20 clerks behind wooden partitions surmounted by wire netting, which ran alongside both sides of the passage. I produced my dearly-bought papers to one of those clerks, but he only smiled and shook his head; they were of no use. He directed me to the far end, where I received a paper exactly (or almost so) similar to those I had, and on which I had to sign my name. When I had done so, the clerk put a few Arabic scrawls on it—I suppose his signature—and handing it to me, called on a porter, who took me to a store and produced the parcel I was in search of. The porter also wanted recompense, but by this time I knew I had been gulled, and indignantly refused. We were alone in the store, and rather than pay more I would fight my way out, so, seizing the parcel, I wrenched it from him and made for the door. He evidently saw that nothing was to be got out of me except by force, which he did not resort to. I was, however, not scot free yet—the duty, 1s. 6d., was to pay. All I had already paid had gone to fatten the pockets of those land sharks. Now, the colonel was done. I had only a 6d. of my own left, and it appeared as if I would have to leave the parcel after all; when one of the clerks suggested that I should see the chief officer of Customs, who might let it go without paying. The suggestion was acted upon, and I was shown into the presence of a nice affable gentleman, who could speak English fluently, and, I have no doubt, many other languages. I explained my position, and handed over my 6d. to him. He said he sympathised with me, as he was himself ashamed of the disgraceful conduct that went on outside the door, and even inside. I asked him how the law did not interfere to prevent such bare-faced open frauds. He smiled, and replied: " Ah, my lad, you little know the corruptness of our laws, or how easily both the law-makers and law-keepers can be bought over; law is almost a dead letter here; but with the assistance of the British Government, and the presence of your country's soldiers (who, I hope, will ever remain with us), things will be put on a better footing, and this abominable cheating done away with." After delivering himself of the above oration, which I wrote down that day, he pulled up the sleeve of his coat, and wrote on his white cuff, Colonel Clery, 1/, saying, that will keep me in mind that he is in my debt. I will see him some day soon.

On my return with the parcel to its master, I gave him the history of my experience. He laughed, and reminded me on the warning he had given before I set out. I suppose he squared his bill with the gentleman who had the account on his cuff—at least I never heard of it again. I went back to the Custom-house often after that, but the same game would not work a second time, and I was allowed to pass on unmolested.

I could recount several more instances of a somewhat similiar kind, but the foregoing is sufficient to give the reader an idea of the swindling that is or was carried on in Alexandria.

Swindling was not all: the lower part of the city, aye and some of the more fashionable parts, stank with immorality. Infamous dens of vice and debauchery existed in almost every street, much more so than in Cairo (which I again visited later on). This being a seaport town, noted for the looseness of both moral and state law, caused the offscourings of almost every nation under the sun to gather in it, and the city seethed with sin.

There is one thing which perhaps the careful reader has observed (and really I cannot account for it), and that is the money-changing on the streets. I have often thought, that had one of those men set their silver and gold-laden table down in a crowded thoroughfare in a British city, what would have been the result. Why, longing eyes would have been cast on it, and if the contents could not be pilfered by stealth, the first opportunity would be seized of upsetting it, and in the *melee* there would be a maddening scramble for the coins. It seems that in this respect, bad as the Alexandria villians are, the villians of our own country are worse. It is, I suppose, a different phase of human nature.

CHAPTER XVI.

CHOLERA IN ALEXANDRIA; ARRIVAL OF COLONEL RICHARDSON AT RAMLEH; PRESENTATION OF EGYPTIAN MEDAL AND STAR.

E had barely occupied the house we had taken possession of on our arrival for a month, when one day a round-faced jolly man of the English county squire type walked in, and demanded to know what right we had in his house. He was, however, in high humour at seeing things in such good order. He having left before the bombardment, had, on his return, expected to see only the blackened ruins of his property. Of course we had to hand over the house, and in the course of a week the offices were removed to the Caracol Attarine, or in English, the police station of the Attarine quarter of the city. I remained there for about six months, during which time the two regiments forming the garrison of Alexandria, viz., Duke of Cornwall's Light Infantry (46), and the West Kent (50) suffered severely through ill health. Enteric fever laid scores of them low, and every day funeral processions were leaving the barracks. It was a trying time for us, to see comrade after comrade carried off with this dreadful fever, and daily we looked for our turn. I had charge of making up the death roll in the office, and for the months of November,

December, and January there was an average of four per day laid in their graves.

The summer advanced, bringing with it the scorching heat of the sun, and also blasts of hot tropical wind. In spite of this, the health of the troops improved, and the continual living in dread expectancy of who would be the next to die began to wear off. But hark! what is this startling report that passes from mouth to mouth, gaining ground every day, causing the inhabitants to shrink shudderingly through the streets, with terror written on every line of their countenance? It was the news that that deadly plague, Asiatic cholera, had spread its destroying wings over the towns in the interior, and was fast nearing Alexandria. For days the people of affluence moved away in a steady stream, as fast as ships could convey them, leaving behind the poor and needy as food for the foul fiend so surely approaching. Soon it laid its hold on the city, and each day scores of men, women, and children were hurried away to their graves. Egyptian funerals poured towards the outer gates, and the air was filled with the lamentations of the mourners.

At an ordinary Egyptian funeral procession the corpse was borne on the shoulders of four men, in a box covered up with a cloth. Men, in pairs, preceded it chanting prayers; but to the women was left the noisiest part. They follow in a group with dishevelled hair, at which they tear and twist, all the time crying and shrieking as if their very hearts were breaking with grief. I often observed that in their frantic gesticulations, when following a corpse, they invariably went through the same motions with the arms as a person would do when driving some animal before them. It looked to me as if they meant: away with the last of this piece of humanity. But all this was dispensed with now; the dead was driven in vans to the cemetery, the followers following afar off in terror.

It was a trying time while the plague lasted. It brought out the different qualities of the human race, soldier and civilian alike. Some waited their time in a sober earnest manner; others flew to drown terror in strong drink, and the city reeked with the reckless orgies of drunken men.

The troops were strictly forbidden to leave the vicinity of the barracks, and on no account to ramble in the town; but we (the head-quarter staff), who were already in the thick of it, and so often compelled by duty to wander in the streets, saw the full extent of the frenzy that reigned. At night fires were lit in the thoroughfares on purpose to purify the air, and though, perhaps, it performed its object, the ghastly flickering of those lurid flames added to the fears of the already terror-stricken people.

In the midst of this turmoil I was promoted to the rank of sergeant, and left the Caracol to rejoin my regiment, which was by this time snugly quartered in barracks, at Ramleh. The railway runs close past the barracks, which were situated on a level, hard sandy piece of ground near the Mediterranean. Close to them stood a handsome palace, then fitted up and occupied as a hospital. Here great precautions were being taken to prevent, if possible, the cholera from spreading. Every morning we scoured the ground in the vicinity, and picked up all of obnoxious refuse that lay about. An Arab village, some 400 yards away, came in for a share of our cleaning, and, for the first time I suppose, the inhabitants saw their lanes swept of their accumulated filth. The only scavengers here were the packs of hungry-looking pariah dogs that hung about the towns and villages in search of food.

The first man who succumbed to the fatal disease was a patient in the hospital; another and another followed. Tents and marquees were pitched, each one at about 100 yards distance from the other, and the whole of the patients were removed and scattered through them.

It was a sight to see the nursing sisters going their rounds in the mornings. They galloped from tent to tent on donkeys, ministering to the wants of the sick with bright smiling faces, that carried a gleam of sunshine to the suffering men, as they smoothed the pillows and soothed the pain with such kindly words as only women can.

The effectual means taken by General Earle (who had relieved General Harman from the command) prevented the spread of the dire plague among the troops, and, with the loss of some 20 men from the Alexandria-Ramleh garrison, it cleared away, and left us in peace.

About this time I was seized with an ophthalmic disease peculiar to Egypt, and by the doctor's orders I was put in a small Indian tent on the hospital plain, and here the first and only night I spent was one of the most miserable nights of my life. The wind blew, causing a sand-storm to arise, and the fine powdery sand whirled and penetrated into my tent in clouds. It irritated my already sore eyes till the pain grew almost unbearable. Bury my head amongst the blankets as I liked, still it found me out. Half mad with agony, I got hold of a shovel that lay in the tent, and went outside to try and prevent its incoming, by shovelling the loose sandy earth against the lower edge of the canvas. But my labour was useless: I might have as well tried to stop the flowing tide. Not a soul was within a 100 yards of me, and in fact my companions might have as well been miles away, for the wind howled so loudly that, even though I had called for assistance, my voice would not have risen above the din of the tempest. Covered, and gradually getting more thickly covered, the night rolled slowly on, and when morning came, I could grasp handfuls of sand from off the pillow; but none could I see, as I was blind, and blind I remained for nearly three weeks. I could not during that time distinguish daylight from darkness. When the doctor arrived, I was removed into the palace, and a comrade along with me for company. For a time I remained in hospital, a helpless and thoroughly disheartened soldier, having been told by the doctors that my eye-sight was partly destroyed, and that too for life. They (luckily for me) proved to be wrong, for in two months I was back to duty as right as ever.

The summer of 1883 was now about at its height, when information came that our colonel had recovered from the wound he had received at Tel-el-kebir, and was on his way to join us. This caused jubilation in the regiment, as he was loved and honoured by all, and more so because since he left, with one thing and another, the behaviour of the battalion had not been of the best. First, the temptations of Alexandria, then the fright of the cholera, had caused many of the men to imbibe too freely, and, as every one knows, when the drink is in the the wit is out, and generally in the long-run misfortune of some kind overtakes the drinker.

The commander that had replaced Colonel Richardson had not the same stern manner, and although severe punishment was administered to evil-doors, there was not the same terror in the administration of it.

We had also come to grief at the hands of the General Earle on inspection day, and from him received only a fair report, as regards drill, and in fact everything else. Therefore the men, who were proud of their regiment, as most soldiers are, hailed the news of Colonel Richardson's return with great joy. One afternoon a message came from Alexandria that he had arrived, and would reach Ramleh by train in about an hour. The word spread from room to room, and, as the time drew near, there was an exodus from the barracks to the small station near by. A few hundreds of us waited outside ready to receive him with a hearty welcome.

Now, I must tell you that mostly every officer and non-commissioned officer, and for that matter the privates too, are the possessors of a nickname, and Colonel Richardson was not exempt. He was familiarly known by the cognomen of " Old Bush " (from what scource derived I know not). Of course the reader will understand that none of us were bold enough to use it in his hearing. But now we were in a crowd, and as the gallant officer, hale and hearty, stepped on to the platform, some one away back called out lustily "three cheers for Old Bush." In a right royal manner the cheers were given, and the smothered laughter when they subsided told how keenly the joke had been relished. The colonel himself took no notice of the name used, and seemed highly gratified with the reception accorded him as he strode on towards the barracks escorted by a heterogenous mob of soldiers.

Arrival of Colonel Richardson at Ramleh. 137

Two days after, he assumed command of the regiment, and his first order was for a parade of all hands. When the companies were formed up, he, mounted on horseback, rode to his old place, and after forming us into a square, addressed us in something like the following terms :—

"My lads, it is a long time since I was at your head, but in that time I have been following your movements, and I have been informed that your behaviour has not been of the best. It has also come to my ears that the general, on last inspection day, said that your drill was not so good as it ought to be. Now, you all know me, and I tell you I will have none of this. Some of you had the impudence to come to the station to meet me, and call three cheers for 'Old Bush.' By heavens! I'll 'Old Bush' you before I am done with you. The general is to inspect you in six weeks, and, if you do not regain your good name on that day, it will be the worse for you, for I will drill you till you wish you had never seen 'Old Bush' again, 'aye.'"

After this crushing speech he put us through a hard hour's drill, and then ordered that each man would get a pint of beer—gratis—at the canteen to drink his health. He well knew the way to gain the soldier's heart: they like nothing better than a good blowing-up on parade from their commander when it finishes up with a pint of beer to wash it down—which generally means that after all he is not in bad humour.

Three or four hours every day we drilled till the day of inspection arrived—not one day but three. The general had changed his opinion, for the third day we were again formed into square to receive an address.

This time a thrill of pride ran through the regiment when we heard General Earle congratulate our colonel on the splendid appearance of his men, concluding his remarks with the words that he would not wish to see a better drilled or better behaved corps in the service. Again the colonel sent us off to get a pint of beer—gratis.

Before we left Ramleh we were presented with the Egyptian medal and star. I remember on reading the account of the same presentation made to regiments that had gone home before they received them. It was a glowing account, and, as a contrast, I will in a few words describe our presentation. The day previous the medals, in small boxes (with the name of the soldier they were intended for written on the lid) were carried round the companies in tin dishes—used for carrying rations and making Irish stews. Each man was told to bring a pin on parade with him on the next day. The Khedive of Egypt was to be there to hand over the medals to the officers.

The appointed hour came. The regiment was formed up, and during the time the Khedive pinned the medals on the breasts of the officers we were busy pinning on our own. A speech from the general followed, and then we prepared to march past. The band (which was left behind at Malta had joined us a while ago) struck up a lively tune, and away went the 19th Hussars past the Ruler of Egypt at a slow trot. Then came the two infantry regiments, our regiment, and the West Kent. There is no doubt we carried our heads high—adorned for the first time with a war medal (a coveted trophy by the soldier), and our pride was pardonable. But the Khedive expressed a wish to see us go past at the trot like the cavalry, so we were marched back to the original starting place, and to the merry music we began to double. One hand had to hold the rifle, the other the bayonet and scabbard, the medals danced on our chests, the pins lost their hold, and, before we got the command to halt, one half of us were minus our medals and stars. It was getting dark ere we got dismissed and back to the parade-ground to gather our lost decorations. Most of the medals were found; and, being made of silver, they were easily seen on the dark brown sand; but the stars, being of bronze, were not so easily detected, and many of them had to lie till morning. A difficulty also arose about the ownership of them, as they bore no distinguishing mark or name and those who were lucky enough to pick up one, it became his own property. This was remedied afterwards by each man's initials and regimental number being stamped on them. In the morning they were all picked up, but, had a sand-storm arisen during the night, I am afraid many of the Egyptian stars would have remained buried amongst Egyptian sand for ever.

CHAPTER XVII.

BACK TO CAIRO.

HRISTMAS season came and went, bringing with it the usual share of rejoicing. Although in a foreign land, and in weather fully as hot as a British summer, we honoured the occasion by holding a big feast in barracks. Soldiers never forget the customs of their own land in whatever clime they roam, more especially if that custom means mirth and feasting.

The news of the doings of the Mahdi or False Prophet in the Soudan were beginning to cause a good deal of excitement in Egypt. The destruction of Hicks Pasha's army on the 5th of November, 1883, had made those wild Soudanese more bold and daring, and in the beginning of the year 1884 they were closing around Suakim.

General Gordon was already on his way to Khartoum to try, with his great influence, to stem the victorious and fanatic wave of the Mahdi's followers. All was again activity, for we were on the eve of another war, and five or six regiments were despatched to Suakim, where, on the 29th February and on March 13th, the battles of El-Teb and Tamai were fought and won by the bravery and dogged determination of British soldiers pitted against hordes of brave savages who gloried in death—their idea being that, if they were killed by the Christians, their spirits were wafted away at once to a land of glorious paradise.

Back to Cairo.

Our regiment was ordered to Cairo, and early one morning, in the month of February, 1884, we packed up our baggage and set out by train. This time we had a pleasant journey; the trucks had disappeared, and in their places were carriages. The distance between the two cities is about 130 miles, but the trains do not go so fast as in our country, and it was late in the afternoon ere we steamed into the station at Cairo. I will not pause to describe the valley that lies between the two principal Egyptian cities, merely remarking that it is a fertile and well cultivated country in its own primitive way. Cotton, corn, and sugar fields stretched away back from the railway on both sides. Palm and fig trees grew in abundance on the banks of numerous canals, which serve as the highways of Egypt. To a person unacquainted with the presence of those water channels, the sight of the tall masts and the broad sails of the dahabeeyehs gliding through the level land causes astonishment, for no water can be seen until close on it. Small towns and villages are abundant on the route, most of the larger being the possessors of a few European buildings, which tend to give an air of more importance to them. Our old acquaintances the Pyramids could be seen on our right front when we were still fifty miles away from them, rising in dim blue masses against the clear sky.

There was a little difference in our appearance this time, as we stood on the station platform of the Egyptian metropolis, than when we stood in the same place nearly two years ago—a few days after the battle of Tel-el-kebir. We had changed our tattered red coats for a suit of grey karkee, it being more adaptable to the climate. There were also amongst us a number who saw Cairo for the first time, as owing to the ravages of disease, principally in the latter months of 1882, and the cholera in the following summer, many had been laid in their graves, and many more were invalided home, while to replace them two drafts had arrived from England. After loading the baggage on to the long narrow lorries, and sending them off with two men in charge of each as a guard, the regiment formed up, and to the martial music of the band, we set out for the citadel, situated at the other end of the city, some three miles from the station. Through streets of greatly different descriptions we marched, some broad and handsome, thickly set with large and well stocked shops, others more of the bye-street type—narrow, dirty, and very squalid. It only required a glance at the passers to convince us that Cairo was a much more Egyptian city than Alexandria. The majority of the people we met were natives, clad in the real Eastern robes. Their gowns, turbans, and sedate countenances reminded me very forcibly of the pictures of men of the days when our Saviour lived on earth, or more remote still, the days when Joseph ruled in Egypt, which pictures can be seen in ancient religious books, and in many family bibles. Those who wore the European garments seemed to have discarded hats in favour of the red tarboush with its big silk tassel.

Carriages, drawn by pairs of horses, whirled along the streets, preceded by two men dressed in fantastic garbs, embroided with imitation gold and silver. They carry a long stick, and run before the carriage, bawling out such words as yemeenák, shimálak, (to the right; to the left). Those fellows will fly on before a swift

Back to Cairo. 143

pair of horses for hours, their bare sinewy legs and feet having an iron look about them.

Strings of camels, laden and unladen, moved slowly along, groaning and grinding their teeth as if they were grumbling at having to work. Seated away high up on the top of the humps sat the drivers, guiding their animals by means of a long stick, with which they tap the brutes on the side of the head furthest from where they want them to go.

Donkeys with richly caparisoned saddles, mounted by men attired in all conceivable modes of dress passed and repassed, followed by the drivers, who prod or strike away at the patient animals, but at once resents if the rider strikes. If a Englishman is on its back, he checks him something after the following manner: "No strikee donkey, Johnny, me strikee plenty."

Such were some of the scenes we saw as we moved on towards the citadel. Before it was dark we had passed through the archway into the main fortress of Cairo. For a day or two we were busy putting things in order, and had no time to look about us; but, as soon as opportunity presented itself, I mounted the ramparts to have a look down upon the town. I remember quite well it was in the evening: the sky was clear, and a splendid sight of the noble city met my gaze. At the first hasty glance one would think the buildings were inconveniently crowded, but, as the eyes wander over it, that thought gradually slips away. The native portion only looks to be one solid mass of grey buildings; the narrowness and shortness of the streets prevents any of the open spaces from being seen from the citadel walls. But the broader streets of the more fashionable quarters, combined with the patches of trees, and acres of pleasure-ground, give an open and refreshing look to that part of the city. Bringing the eye to gaze on the nearer thoroughfares, a conglomeration of men, women, camels, donkeys, and dogs moved along in a mixed throng. I was struck with the erect and graceful carriage of the women—the working women. The habit of carrying pitchers of water and other things on their heads, without the aid of hands, has imparted to them an attidude that a grenadier would be proud of. Close to the gate below, donkeys and donkey-boys waited for the out-coming of the British soldiers for their evening's enjoyment, and, as they appeared in twos and threes, a scramble immediately arose among the lads to get them to appropriate their donkeys, and the good qualities of the quadrupeds were loudly eulogized by their respective drivers, in something like the terms already mentioned as used at Alexandria. Close to the citadel were the principal mosques, two in particular, one at the foot of the hill, the other on the same hill, but a few hundred yards south of the citadel. Their minarets tower high up into the sky; but, as high as they are, almost every night the "Mueddins" (the men who call the worshippers to prayer) can be heard away some where about the top bawling out what was to us gibberish, but no doubt an exhortation to his countrymen to betake themselves to their worship.

At particular seasons of the year great religious ceremonies are solemnised, and it is at this time that the mosques are most patronised. I never had the pleasure of entering one; but several times have I stood watching the crowds flowing in and out, and they were not solemn crowds either. Bands of Ghazeeyehs or dancing girls hung about the entrance, their well moulded forms displayed to advantage, and their handsome faces dancing with mirth. They were not slack at even seizing the British soldier, if he passed near them, in an endearing hug, amid the merry laughter of their companions. It always seemed to me that, in place of religious ceremonies, those periodical feasts and fasts assumed the same shape as a day of rejoicing over some great event would in our own land. On those occasions the minarets of the mosques were lighted up by a perfect multitude of lamps, and the men at the top annoyed the whole neighbourhood with their "Allahs and Akbars;" while far beneath them the town was alive with processions, and music of tambourines, Egyptian pipes (which, by the by, have a sound somewhat resembling Scotch bagpipes), drums, kettle-drums, flutes, &c.

For about three months we remained in Cairo, with very little to do but stroll about the city and enjoy ourselves. We found the amusements somewhat the same as at Alexandria. One thing that at once strikes the sojourner in this city is the amount of buying and selling that is carried on in the streets. Fruit, fowls, eggs, flowers, &c., are hawked about—the sellers calling out the good qualities of their articles, and generally demanding three times the price they are prepared to sell them for, if the buyer is foolish enough to give it.

"Sakkas" or water-carriers are numerous; they hobble along with a goat's skin full of water on their back, holding the narrow end. They sell to the householders, and likewise are often employed to water the streets and the avenues of the fine residences. There is another class of water-carriers who carry on their backs a large earthenware pitcher with a long brass or tin spout. From them you may buy a drink, and it is surprising how they can hold the small dish they carry, and, by slightly bending their body forward, allow the water to rush from the spout over their shoulders into it without spilling a drop. Then there is the " Liquorice Man," who goes clattering two little brass saucers in his hand, calling " Liquorish "—a reddish coloured sweet-tasting beverage.

Before leaving Cairo I should like to take the readers with me on an evening's ramble through the streets, in the hope that I may leave them with a slight impression of the scenes which are to be met with only in this the capital of Egypt.

Leaving the barracks about 5 p.m. we saunter into the city, following the turnings and twistings of broad streets, set with shops and grand mansions surrounded by grounds studded with trees, plants, and bushes—all of oriental beauty. The murmur of splashing water in the fountains conveys to us a pleasant sensation after the intense heat of a summer day.

Here comes a troop of donkeys, and their drivers are shouting for our patronage. We select what we think the best and swiftest. On to the saddle we jump, and are borne along at an ambling gallop. The whole street is one movable panorama. We pass ladies closely veiled, with only their black eyes to be seen. Camels, heavily laden, troop growlingly past, mounted by old grisly-bearded natives, black slaves, and copper-coloured Soudanese, &c. Donkeys gallop hither and thither, ridden by people of all ages and various nations, dressed in all sorts of costumes, from the flowing robes of the rich Egyptian (male and female) and the smarter dress of the European to the almost nude Arab. Turning a corner we hear the

Back to Cairo.   147

guttural cry of a running footman, and we know to clear the way. Past us dash, at full gallop, a number of carriages, from the windows of which we get a glimpse of the damsels of some nobleman's harem. Europeans on horseback, donkey back, and on foot, press through the moving crowds with an air of hurry, as much as to say "get out of the way, you are too slow for me." But what is this moving armoury coming towards us ? It is a party of Albanians and Bashi-Bazouks dressed in their fantastic garb. A broad cloth band is twisted round their loins, into the folds of which pistols, revolvers, and large-handled, long-bladed knives are stuck in profusion.

Turning from the principal thoroughfare, we enter a narrow street, and before we are aware we gaze around on what looks like the interior of a roofless boot factory. On both sides of the street, boots and shoes of all shapes and sizes are heaped on the narrow footway; while beside them sit the sellers, indolently smoking a long pipe, with an air of "buy if you please." We are in the boot and shoe bazaar.

Hardly have we left the shoe bazaar behind when, on rounding a corner, our eyes are fascinated with the sight of hundreds of richly-embroidered carpets and rugs, hanging in one beautiful and bewildering maze. What a lovely and animated scene: all the colours of the rainbow are here intermixed. Turbaned natives, tarboushed Europeans, on foot and on horse and donkey-back, are seething through this lane of gorgeous splendour. The air is filled with the hum of many voices, some in the angry-like altercation of bargain-making, others in friendly conversation; but it is only by their looks that we judge, for it is all gibberish to us. Our donkeys slowly and surely forge ahead through the noisy throng, and, with all its picturesque loveliness, we are glad when we reach the outer edge of this—the carpet bazaar.

But, hark! the rollicking sound of Egyptian music is wafted to our ears, and we have to press close to the walls to allow a bridal procession to pass. Men, youths, women, and maidens, all in the flowing garb of Egypt, formed in threes and fours, move along, carrying proudly above them several square silken banners. A crowd follows, and, for a few minutes, we grasp the saddle, and our donkeys sway with the pressure until it passes. Many other bazaars we visit, containing rare and beautiful articles, too numerous to mention, and, with our heads in a maze, we ride on.

After this, we must have refreshments, and, turning the donkeys' heads in the direction of the European quarter, we push on, and in a short time dismount, pay our fares, and enter a large handsome hall. Small marble tables are there in scores, and we take our seats on some of the chairs placed beside them. Ordering our beer or whatever else we want, and flavouring it with a piece of ice, we lay back to hear a tune or two. On a stage, at the far end of the hall, sit about a score of lovely damsels (forming the band), and delighting the already large audience with the sweet strains of their numerous instruments. A few tunes and a few glasses suffice us, and we leave on purpose to get an evening glimpse of a thorough native street. Entering a narrow lane, as black as night itself, along which we cautiously tread our way until a blaze of light appears a short distance ahead. On coming up to it, we have to pick our way carefully through a score or more of small tables, at which a number of the real slum Egyptians are seated. They hate the very sight of us, and their scowling looks plainly say: "Get out of here." We take the hint and leave; for an eerie feeling creeps over us at the darkness of the streets and the murderous looks of those swarthy men. Back to more congenial scenes we hie, but, before going back to barracks, we must have one more rest. Leaving the street, we pass up a few steps, and find ourselves under a clump of palm trees, hanging on which are a number of many-coloured lanterns. Seating ourselves at a table close to a sparkling fountain, we partake of another iced beer or lemonade.

On leaving this, we run tilt against a crowd, which almost blocks the street. What is it? Our natural curiosity prompts us to push forward and see. Elbowing our way to the centre, there, in an open space, stands a "Hawee" or sleight-of-hand performer, who are to be seen by the score in Cairo. Those men and women (for both sexes perform) do some wonderfully clever and astonishing tricks. This one is, when we see him first, pulling yards of thread from his mouth, and a companion is winding it up. It seems, as the ball gets bigger and bigger, as if the man belonged to the spider species. When he has spun enough to satisfy the crowd that he could not have held it all in his mouth, he began blowing silver coins from his nose. Then he produced a small box, and after showing all present that it was empty, closed the lid, and muttered a few words quite unintelligible to us; then opening the lid, he pulled from the box a large white rabbit. But we had seen those tricks, or similar ones, so often before that they were no novelty to us, so, hiring a donkey each, we set out, and had a rattling race for first at the barrack gate.

In all honesty I must make one more remark regarding Cairo, and that is, that it is not such a crime-ridden or swindling city as Alexandria. Being away from the sea-board line, the worst type of foreigners do not patronise it in such large numbers.

We did not remain in the citadel during the whole of our stay in Cairo, but spent a short time in Kasr-Nil Barracks. Those barracks consist of two massive blocks, forming three sides of two squares, the broad flowing Nile sweeping past in front forming the fourth side. The bridge spanning the river was close by, and directly opposite was the sandy plain where we encamped, when on our first visit. The interiors of those magnificent buildings were fitted up in a style similar to barrack-rooms at home; and had it not been for the broad verandahs of the three-storied blocks, and the stairs placed only at the corners instead of up through the inside, there was little difference on our quarters from the barracks in an English or Scotch city. The Royal Highlanders (Black Watch) occupied one of the squares, and as a number of the men who had been at the festivities between my former regiment (the 1st Battalion Duke of Cornwall's Light Infantry), in the year 1880, at Aldershot, were still alive, a sort of good-fellowship sprung up, and what with cricket matches between different companies, and feasting each other, the two regiments spent many a jolly evening together.

CHAPTER XVIII.

FROM CAIRO TO ASSOUAN.

E had a regular supply of home papers, though not exactly up to date, being about a week old ere they reached us. In them we could see that troubles were already brewing in the Soudan, and long paragraphs about the desirability of sending troops up the Nile became more and more frequent. It also seemed as if the Duke of Cornwall's Light Infantry were not destined to stay long in one place, for in the month of June the order came to pack up and proceed to Kenneh, a small mud town 400 miles further south, and nearer the frontier of Egypt. Leaving all our baggage in a store at Kasr-Nil Barracks, we marched across the bridge to a railway station in the Gezeereh district, about two miles off, taking with us one extra suit of clothing, and complete camp equipment.

The first 200 miles of our journey was by rail, which occupied a whole day and night, and it was far into the second day before we arrived at the town of Assiout, which is situated at the terminus of the railway. I was much surprised at the appearance of the country we had passed through. The railway runs almost within full view of the Nile the whole way, and instead of the miles of sand and desert we had expected to see, acres upon acres of richly cultivated land extended along the banks of this broad flowing, historic, and wonderful river. One difference I observed was the absence of canals ; but they were not wanted, as the cultivated soil was only at the most a mile in width, and was all watered by irrigation from the river itself. There are divers means of conducting this irrigation process—according to the wealth of the owners. The poor Egyptian uses a very simple and inexpensive machine, if I may call it so, to water his few acres. It consists of two posts of wood, or in some cases two piles of hardened mud, about five feet high, placed on the bank near the water's edge. Across the top of those uprights is fixed a round stick, about six inches in diameter, both ends of which are secured by being built over with mud baked into a solid mass by the heat of the sun. A branch of a tree, about 15 feet long, is fastened to the cross bar, so as to act as a lever, in "see-saw" style. A heavy lump of hard mud is cloated round the end furthest from the water, and to the opposite end is tied a rope with a bowel-shaped bucket, or rather basket, for it seemed to be wickerwork. This is called a shadoof. To work it, a man (naked, except a band round his loins, and sometimes devoid even of that) stands on a platform cut out in the muddy bank near the top. He pulls down the rope, thereby bringing the end of the lever with it, until the bucket touches the water, then, giving it a clever cant, it fills itself. Slackening his hold, up comes the bucket by means of the heavy mud on the other end of lever. As soon as it comes within reach of the man, he seizes and empties it into the prepared channel, from whence it spreads over the land. At some places, where the river's banks are high, as many as three of those shadoofs are required—the lower two filling a sort of reservoir, and the upper one discharging the water on to the land. Some of them are double-barrelled, so to speak, they having two levers on the one cross bar, and a man working each with exact regularity. This work must be disagreeable, for it makes a sort of creeping shudder come over one to see those naked fellows standing on the wet soft mud, dripping from head to foot with what is spilled from their basket buckets. All day long there they stand at their cheerless task—really a miserable life for daily bread.

There is another style of machine for the same purpose, the owner of it being endowed with a larger share of wordly goods than the shadoof owner. It is called a sakiyeh. A couple of oxen are required to drive it, and round and round they go like horses in a threshing mill, often to be seen about a Scotch farm. By this means a few ricketty wooden wheels are set in motion, and the water is brought up by a number of earthenware jars tied on to a continuous rope. As those jars pass through the water they fill, and, as they pass over the top, out flows the water into the ditch prepared for it. Those sakiyehs have a most disagreeable creaking noise, and, on the way to Kenneh in the steamers, if we lay-to for the night, in the vicinity of one of them, sleep was next to impossible.

We passed a few handsome farm steadings about half-way to Assiout, and their appearance, coupled with the construction of the dwelling-houses, standing at a distance, showed that an Englishman or Scotchman had settled there.

On leaving the train we saw that preparations had been made for us, three of Cook's steamers (of tourist world-wide fame) lying waiting. Little time was lost: it was all hands strip and work, till everything was on board, and then we took up our quarters on deck, which served as table, promenade, and bed. The seamen, or, to be nearer the mark, rivermen, unloosed the fastenings, and out on the broad and winding river we floated *en route* for Kenneh.

We did not get an opportunity of visiting the town of Assiout, but we could see it from the vessel, standing away back from the river about half a mile. It looked a large and thickly set town, for the minarets of a goodly number of mosques rose clear and distinct above the sky-line of the desert behind. Here the river was about, I should say, 1000 yards in width, and bending away round to the left.

It was a dull time on this our first Nile voyage. For days no sound save the incessant splash of the paddles broke the stillness, as we lay stretched on the decks under the welcome shade of an awning during the fierce blaze of the sun. The same monotonous scenery greeted us as turn after turn of the river was winded through. Sometimes narrow patches of cultivation and clumps of magnificent palms met our gaze. At other times we were steaming between mountains of sand and limestone, extending from the river's edge as far back as the eye could see. When we were close to those greyish white hills it was painful to look on them, the rays of the tropical sun dazzling the eyes. I observed that on the eastern bank these mountains were most numerous and largest, and in many of them, away up near the summit, could be seen dark frowning holes, evidently the mouths of caverns and tombs, the relics of ancient Egypt. Small villages were abundant, and it was a matter of speculation amongst us where the inhabi-

From Cairo to Assouan. 155

tants got work or a living. There seemed to be nothing to depend on but the narrow strips of cultivation where they grew vegetables and fruit, such as onions, beans, melons, dates, grapes, &c. I should imagine beef was an unknown luxury to those brown, sun, and climate-burned natives However, they seemed to grow and thrive without it, as the further we went, the more athletic and supple grew both males and females.

Five or six days brought us to Girgeh, a town on the west bank, where the steamers took in a supply of coal. We also got the opportunity of taking in a supply of vegetables, fruit, fowls, and eggs, and even some of their half buffalo, half bullock meat, which, though uncommonly tough, and not eaten to any extent by themselves, proved a welcome change to our daily ration of tinned beef. A few hours sufficed to coal the steamers, and on we went again, arriving in Kenneh in a few more days. Here we disembarked with all our belongings, and pitched our tents under the shade of a grove of palm trees, near the water's edge.

Just a few words about Kenneh, seeing that we remained there for about two months. It was composed of a lot of small dingy mud hovels, planted hither and thither, without any semblance of regularity, on a piece of high-lying, hard, sandy soil, a few hundred yards from the river proper, but close to the water, as, owing to the Nile sweeping away to the right, the outside angle flooded a part of the low-lying ground, close up to the mound on which the village stood. There was only one industry carried on, and that was the making of earthenware filters, pitchers, jars, and "chatties." Piles of them lay on the vacant spaces between the houses, while a number of dahabeeyehs were loading and leaving for Cairo every day with cargoes of those useful articles. One thing I observed at Kenneh, which is very rare at towns on the Nile, and that was, several towers, about a mile inland, adorned with large white painted wind-mills. For what purpose they were used I never found out, as it was a matter of difficulty to get any information. Not a soul, except ourselves, in the place could speak or understand English, except the regimental interpreter. We managed to purchase fruit and vegetables by signs, and also an occasional bottle of " con-ē ak," as Kenneh, besides its industry, could boast of two mud huts, wherein spirits of an abominable kind were sold. Very few, who get tipsy once, took much of it at any future period, as the dire effects of its poisonous nature tortured the inner man for days. A mail steamer sailed once a week to and from Assouan, and letters and papers came with it regularly. For the latter we are indebted to ladies and gentlemen in our own country, many of whom sent a weekly supply, for which, in our hearts, we gratefully thanked them. Those acts of kindness came as a spring shower in this land of sand-storms and broiling sun.

We were not destined to stay long here, neither were we sorry. Better be on the move, even though it were to a worse place, than remain idle and half roasted at Kenneh. So we hailed with joy the order to get ready to go on board the steamers and barges that would call for us in a few days. By the month of August, 1884, we were again stretched on the decks listlessly whiling away the time, as our vessels slowly beat their way against stream, bound for Assouan. We passed that historic part of the Nile where the wondrous ruins of Thebes stand majestically on both banks of the river. High walls and monuments, to all appearance of enormous size and strength, grown grey and battered by the hand of father time, looked across to us, and we longed to explore them; but we were not a pleasure party, and had to be content with a passing glance. On the east bank rose the Temple of Karnak, standing back from the Nile a little way, and had it not been that our steamer touched the bank for some reason or other, and remained for about a quarter of an hour, thus giving us an opportunity of running ashore on to higher ground, we might have passed those old temple walls and columns without being any the wiser.

About a mile further on we came to the town of Luxor. It stands on the east bank, and close to the softly flowing water. The inhabitants of this place showed more signs of friendliness than those of any of the other towns we had as yet passed. It could also boast of a hotel, above the door of which hung a signboard bearing the words "Luxor Hotel," with the name of the owner, also in English, painted above the door. How refreshing even the letters looked, and we spelled and pronounced the name time after time. I think it was the sight of this signboard that made us raise a hearty cheer to the assembled natives as we glided past. In return, the British flag was run up above the hotel. This brought another deafening cheer from us. Many of the inhabitants followed along the banks, almost touching the vessel, so near the side did we sail, our steersman evidently knowing where to go for deep water. The natives were displaying copies of the New Testament, and calling out that they were Christians, at the same time asking for "bucksheesh" for adopting our religion. Several missionaries were established here, and their labours were, to all appearance, not in vain, and in time they may stamp out the eternal cry of "bucksheesh" from the true religion which they are trying to instil into those simple-minded, quiet, inoffensive people of Luxor.

The temple of the god Ammon stands in the centre of the town, also close on the river's brink, and the passing view of it we got revealed a number of vast round columns of greyish stone, profuse with carving. All those ruins we had seen kept the mind running away back to the days we had read of, when Moses and the Pharoahs of Egypt lived and moved through the land, for those grand old structures were too mighty and useless to belong to our period of civilisation.

A few miles above Luxor we passed a large sugar factory, the first building of anything like modern appearance we had sighted since we left Cairo. On our arrival at Esneh, a town of considerable importance, we called for a supply of coal, and, while some were bartering with the inhabitants for supplies of fowls and vegetables, as a change to the everlasting bully-beef, others were amusing themselves throwing coins and other articles into the muddy river on purpose to see the natives diving and fetching them to the surface. This they could and did do with little trouble. They seemed to be as much at home in the Nile as on its banks. We got a ration of fresh beef, but potatoes were unknown; we had not seen any for months.

About nine days' steady steaming brought us to Assouan, where we disembarked, and, selecting a grove of palm trees, we pitched our camp under its welcome shade.

Assouan is a mud village, boasting of about 1000 inhabitants. It is situated 600 miles south of Cairo, on the frontier of Egypt, and near to the first cataract, which blocks the further progress of steamers. The huts are built on a sandy waste, close to the water. Hills of sand and rock stretch away to the southward. A few of the now familiar ruins raise their grey time-battered walls and columns in the vicinity. The green island of Elphantine lies in the very centre of the river, which has the effect of widening it to some 1200 yards. Stunted palm trees, growing in scattered groups, and small patches of cultivated land, slightly enliven the barren and gloomy surroundings of this frontier village. Here we had to stay for a few months among mosquitoes, flies, scorpions, lizards, and last but not least, whirlwinds and sand storms. Here, on the verge of thousands of miles of the Soudan desert, and also on the eve of one of the most arduous and difficult tasks that ever the British army was called upon to perform, viz., the ascent of the rock-studded, torrent-tossed Nile, I will bid farewell to my readers. At some future time I may take them up this mighty river for hundreds of miles, through foaming cataracts and rushing rapids. But the toils and dangers of that ascent are too varied and numerous to be adequately described within the pages of this book. Therefore, readers, "One and All" (the motto of the Duke of Cornwall's Light Infantry), at present I say, Adieu!

THE END.

PRINTED AT THE ABERDEEN JOURNAL OFFICE.

www.ingramcontent.com/pod-product-compliance
Lightning Source LLC
Chambersburg PA
CBHW030403100426
42812CB00028B/2811/J